ECCLESIASTICAL CRAFTS

BUCKY KING / JUDE MARTIN

VNR **VAN NOSTRAND REINHOLD COMPANY**
New York   Cincinnati   Toronto   London   Melbourne

For Wilbur and John-David

For Don

Copyright © 1978 by Van Nostrand Reinhold Company
Library of Congress Catalog Card Number 77-25033
ISBN 0-442-22966-6

Printed in the United States of America
Designed by Loudan Enterprise
Published in 1978 by Van Nostrand Reinhold Company
A division of Litton Educational Publishing, Inc.
135 West 50th Street, New York, NY 10020, U.S.A.

Van Nostrand Reinhold Limited
1410 Birchmount Road
Scarborough, Ontario M1P 2E7, Canada

Van Nostrand Reinhold Australia Pty. Ltd.
17 Queen Street
Mitcham, Victoria 3132, Australia

Van Nostrand Reinhold Company Limited
Molly Millars Lane
Wokingham, Berkshire, England

16 15 14 13 12 11 10 9 8 7 6 5 4 3 2 1

Library of Congress Cataloging in Publication Data

King, Bucky.
  Ecclesiastical crafts.

  Bibliography: p. 128
  Includes index.
  1. Liturgical objects. 2. Church vestments.
3. Christian art and symbolism. 4. Church
decoration and ornament. I. Martin, Jude, joint
author. II. Title.
NK1650.K47   745.5   77-25033
ISBN 0-442-22966-6

CONTENTS

ACKNOWLEDGEMENTS/4

INTRODUCTION/5

Chapter 1. SYMBOLISM IN RELIGIOUS ART/6

Chapter 2. ECCLESIASTICAL APPOINTMENTS/24

Chapter 3. THE CLERGY AND THE CRAFTSMAN—FINDING THE CRAFTSMAN FOR THE JOB/49

Chapter 4. THE CRAFTSMAN AND THE CLERGY—OPPORTUNITIES FOR THE CRAFTSMAN/52

Chapter 5. CERAMICS IN ECCLESIASTICAL CRAFTS/55

Chapter 6. ENAMEL AND METAL IN ECCLESIASTICAL CRAFTS/64

Chapter 7. FIBER IN ECCLESIASTICAL CRAFTS/82

Chapter 8. WOOD IN ECCLESIASTICAL CRAFTS/118

Chapter 9. WHEN, WHERE, WHAT, AND WHY/126

BIBLIOGRAPHY/128

INDEX/130

ACKNOWLEDGEMENTS

In compiling this book, we have contacted hundreds of people both by direct mail, surveys, and through quarterly publications. We wish to thank Barbara Brabec of "Artisan Crafts" and Marilyn Heise of "The Working Craftsman," who were among the editors who published our plea to craftsmen in their magazines. We sent form letters to forty-two craft guilds throughout the country, who published our plea for contact with their members. For technical assistance, we are indebted to The Most Reverend Robert B. Appleyard, Episcopal Bishop of the Diocese of Pittsburgh, and Dr. Solomon B. Freehof, rabbi of Rodelf Shalom Temple.

Printing, survey, and mailing costs were partly defrayed by a grant from the Foothills Craft Guild, Oak Ridge, Tennessee.

We thank each of the craftsmen who sent material, photographs, or work and have been so patient and encouraging along the way.

A special thank you must go to Susan Rosenthal and Nancy Newman Green of Van Nostrand Reinhold for all their contributions and help.

INTRODUCTION

In recent years a number of books have been written on the subjects of Hebrew art and crafts, Byzantine crafts, Egyptian tomb artifacts, Chinese religious and symbolic art, and American Indian art and crafts. All these art forms are directly involved with sacred beliefs of the people who created them and are in a sense liturgical forms of expression.

Little exposure has been given in the Judeo-Christian heritage to contemporary liturgical crafts and the ever-broadening field this encompasses. Certainly there are more books on Jewish art forms than there are on Christian-oriented liturgical art, although specific branches of Christianity have traditionally endeavored to promote and encourage ecclesiastical art. In the pages and photos presented here we hope to spark your interest in the area of liturgical crafts.

Many churches and synagogues today continue to present liturgical symbols which are outdated for our time and way of life. The great cathedrals of bygone eras presented magnificent art and crafts to the worshippers, and the tradition of the craft guilds during the Middle Ages promoted work of great excellence. Unfortunately, much of this beauty of design and craftsmanship has been watered down by the numerous "copies" which are mass-produced today and passed off as religious art. There seems to be a void in religious art, both in education and the artwork itself.

The liturgical crafts presented here are directly related to specific houses of worship to serve purposeful functions. We hope that they will inspire clergy, congregations, and craftsmen to revitalize the partnership of religion and art.

CHAPTER 1.

SYMBOLISM IN RELIGIOUS ART

The *Shorter Oxford Dictionary* defines a symbol as "something that stands for, represents, or denotes something else, not by exact resemblance but by vague suggestion. An object representing something sacred." The practice of using visual symbols for religious purposes was started in biblical times and further developed by both Christians and Jews over the centuries. In religious symbolism color, line, and form are mingled together to make a visual impression. This impression has the power to communicate ideas and feelings; symbolic art should convey vitality, but most importantly, it should illuminate the faith for succeeding generations. Outgrowths of the complex interaction between life, faith, and belief, religious symbols become a language without words, binding together those of the same religion or culture.

Today many artists and craftsmen are aware of a need for a new symbolism to develop—one that reflects our own age and time. Surprisingly enough, while modern man lives within a world highly composed of symbols, he presently has no symbols for such concepts as joy, prayer, hope, and kindness. The potential for the development of a new symbolism in religion by the artist or craftsman is tre-

mendous. Entire volumes have been written on the subject of religious symbolism alone, so we cannot begin to cover it in detail here. We will, however, discuss the use of color as a symbol and some of the already existing religious symbols.

COLOR

Color itself is a symbol in religious art. In Exod. 26:1 we learn that the curtains for the Temple were to be made of purple, blue, and scarlet finely twined linen. No one knows why these four colors were designated for use in the great Tent of Meeting, but, beginning in Exodus, chapter 25, God gives detailed instructions to Moses regarding its construction. The specifications included acacia wood, gold, silver, brass, and the four colors; even the craftsmen were selected. Later on in the Bible, the splendors of Solomon's Temple in Jerusalem are said to be exceeded by Herod's temple. In fact, the early books of the Old Testament are a history of temple building with detailed instructions for many articles used therein. Hebrew liturgical color was once confined to the four colors—purple, blue, scarlet, and natural-colored linen—plus gold and silver, but now there is no restriction in color use. In fact, colors have developed their own symbolic meanings that are associated with the change in Jewish or Christian seasons. A liturgical color chart for both Christianity and Judaism follows to show the variety of colors used from medieval times to the present and how they've changed. Many colors come to have special meanings or contradictory meanings. White, for example, was used as the color for mourning in the fourteenth and fifteenth centuries, rather than black.

The colors most often used for religious purposes are listed on page 8. Remember that they are done in many varieties of tone and value. All of the color principles of harmony, balance, and dominance still apply to whatever hue is used, regardless of its symbolic meaning; a red shade must harmonize with a blue or green shade used in order to create a total color symphony.

Liturgical Color Chart

Festival	Present Color		Medieval Variations
	Roman and Anglican Churches	*Other Denominations*	
Advent	purple violet blue	blue	black red white
Christmas	white	red	red gold brown
St. Stephen	red	red	not known
St. John, the Evangelist	white	white	not known
Holy Innocents' Day	red	red	not known
Circumcision	white	white	not known
Epiphany	white or red	red	gold yellow green
Septuagesima to Lent	green violet blue	red blue	red blue black
Ash Wednesday	red	blue	red blue
Lent	purple violet	unbleached linen	red blue white

Festival	Present Color		Medieval Variations
	Roman and Anglican Churches	Other Denominations	
Palm Sunday and Maundy Thursday	red	red	not known
Good Friday	black purple red	purple red	ash color
Easter	white	white	red green purple
Pentecost or Whitsuntide	white	white	gold purple brown
Trinity Sunday	white	red	red green purple gold
Trinity to Advent	green	red or green	violet gold blue
Yom Kippur		white	
Rosh Hashanah		white	

Common Symbolic Colors

White: The color of life and purity; used by many denominations on important holy days.

Gold: The symbol of the divine or celestial light and the glory of God.

Silver: The symbol for innocence and holiness.

Red: The symbol for life, blood, and fire.

Green: The color of nature, symbolizing how God provides for man's needs.

Purple and Blue: The symbol of penance and purification of sin; also royalty.

Black: The symbol of death and mourning.

ARTICLES

Down through the centuries thousands of artists and craftsmen have produced symbolic art for purposes of worship and religious ornamentation. The following are some of the most common articles, and are offered for suggestion only. They by no means exhaust the countless possibilities, past or present, that come under the heading of symbolic religious art.

Traditional Religious Symbolic Articles

The Tree of Life: A reminder of the Garden of Eden, the "Etz Chayyim" often adorns menorahs, doors, book bindings, chalices, ciboria, hangings, and Torah mantels. It is basically a traditional tree or vine form, either mimicking nature or abstracted as a main line with accompanying branch lines. It can be done in many styles and forms with unlimited design potential. This symbol is used in both Christianity and Judaism.

The Cross: This is the recognized symbol of Christianity. The crucifix, which is a representation of Christ on the cross, symbolizes his passion. The cross can take hundreds of design forms and shapes. New ones are just waiting to be created.

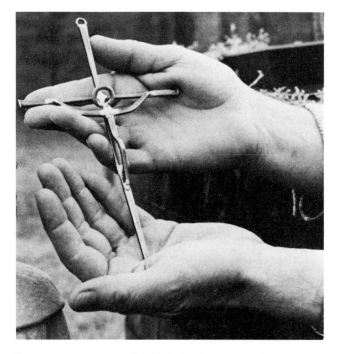

Figure 1-1. "Crucifix." This 8- by 4-inch crucifix was made with nails that were braze-welded together. Designed and executed by J. J. Sokolovich. Courtesy of Bucky King. Photographed by Ruth Carey.

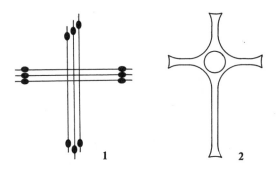 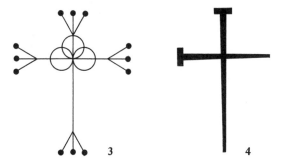

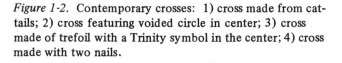

Figure 1-2. Contemporary crosses: 1) cross made from cattails; 2) cross featuring voided circle in center; 3) cross made of trefoil with a Trinity symbol in the center; 4) cross made with two nails.

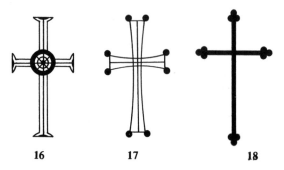

Figure 1-3. Crosses; 1) Latin cross; 2) Greek cross; 3) Tau cross; 4) cross Potent; 5) St. Andrew's cross; 6) voided Greek cross; 7) crosslet; 8) cross of Lorraine; 9) Jerusalem or Crusader's cross; 10) Papal cross; 11) Ansated cross; 12) Russian cross; 13) Patriarchal cross; 14) the cross and circle; 15) Flyfoot or Swastika cross; 16) the Celtic cross; 17) Byzantine-style cross; 18) cross botonée with trefoil buds.

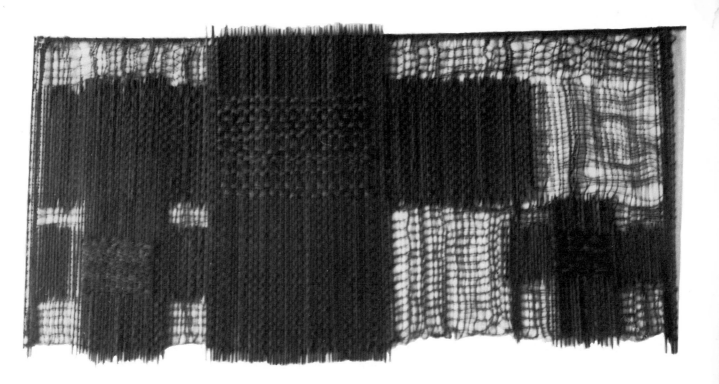

Figure 1-4. "Calvary." This 11- by 19-inch wall hanging was woven with wool and reeds. The three crosses in the design represent the scene at the Crucifixion. Designed and executed by Marjorie Pohlman. Photographed by Charles Pohlman.

The Menorah: In Judaism lights are kindled every Sabbath. Light itself symbolizes many things—knowledge, truth, justice, our aspirations to the eternal, and God's radiance in this world. The menorah is a seven-branched candelabra, which represents the creation of the universe in seven days. It is used exclusively in Judaism. The Sabbath is represented by the center light, which in turn symbolizes guidance by the light of God. The menorah can take many forms. However, it is frowned upon to make an exact copy of the menorah used in the Temple of Jerusalem.

The Trinity: There are many symbols for the Trinity, including the triangle, the three rings, and the three crowns. The Trinity represents the three-fold nature of God—Father, Son, and Holy Spirit—one in substance, but three in individuality. Design forms using three-part ideas can be created to form hundreds of new symbols to express this concept.

Images of Christ: The challenge to represent Christ has been taken up by many artists using all types of materials. Using the image of Christ to remind people of his death and passion has been done since the early years of Christianity, and it still remains a challenge for the artist today. These images of Christ tell stories or guide the mind to biblical passages recorded in the Gospels. Images of Christ fall into two major divisions—those depicting events in his life as recorded in the Gospels and those representing celestial power or divine compassion.

The Virgin Mary: Mary, the mother of Christ, is represented in many ways. She is often shown as a female figure adorned in blue with a halo over her head; she represents the mother image in Christianity. She is frequently depicted as the madonna holding the Christ child and is always represented in the Nativity, as well as in many of the story–telling scenes or pictures taken from the Gospels.

The Nativity: The birth of Jesus is a favorite symbol during the Christmas and Epiphany seasons. The Nativity symbolizes the new light in the world introduced by the birth of Christ and offers a huge range of design potential, since many figures are involved in the scene. Included usually are Mary, Joseph, the Wise Men, the Christ child, and the animals in the stable. The scene has universal appeal among children.

The Eternal Light: This light hangs over the holy ark in synagogues and is always kept burning. It has been described as an emblem of the twelve tribes of Israel, symbolizing the unity of the people of Israel. Undoubtedly, the practice of continually burning the light comes from the early practice in the first temples of allowing one lamp, the "Ner ha Ma'a-ravi," "Lamp of God," to burn all day, refilling it in the evening and from it lighting all the other lamps. The Eternal Light, or "Ner Tamid" can take many forms and designs. It is still used in many Christian houses of worship as well.

The Holy Ark: In synagogues the ark is the tabernacle that houses the Torah, or scroll of the law. It is the supreme symbol in Judaism, representing the tabernacle in Solomon's Temple; this sanctity was transferred to the Holy Ark and the Torah within. There are as many different designs for arks as there are synagogues.

Water: Water is the symbol for baptism, since Christ was baptized in water. It is often used on baptismal fonts in a symbolic pattern of wavy lines.

The Holy Spirit: The Holy Ghost is the third person in the Trinity concept. It represents the spirit of God in the world and is often depicted as an ascending or descending dove. The hand of God, extended, is often a symbol for the Holy Spirit, as are the burning bush or tongues of fire.

Figure 1-5. The menorah, made of unglazed red clay, is 16 inches tall and 16½ inches wide at the top. Designed and executed by Riva H. Freed. Courtesy of Mrs. Shirley Shuman.

Figure 1-6. Trinity symbols: 1) triangle with three distinct equal angles; 2) the trefoil, which are three connected but distinct circles, used by St. Patrick for the Trinity symbol; 3) the Petragram, or five-pointed star; 4) Trinitas Unitas, which is three interlocked circles; 5) the triquetra, which is the interweaving of three equal arcs; 6) three triangles joined to make one figure; 7) the fork with three lines coming to a single point; 8) a contemporary leaf in three parts.

The Eucharist: This is the universal symbol for Holy Communion, or the Lord's Supper. It can be represented in many ways, such as a wine cup and a loaf of bread, a chalice and a wafer, images of the Last Supper, grapes and wheat for wine and bread, loaves and fish, or simply the colors of red and white.

Figure 1-7. "Fishes and Loaves." This wall hanging combines techniques of appliqué, embroidery, and quilting. The work measures 37 by 48 inches. Designed and executed by Deborah Anderson. Photographed by Jim Rodgers.

Figure 1-8. The top winged angel was taken from carvings in the tenth-century church in Oshki, Russia. These carvings may be early forerunners of those found in European churches of the Romanesque period. The angel at the bottom is a more contemporary one.

14

Angels: Angels are used to represent God's messengers to earth. The winged angel is a symbol of celestial power and protection. It is used in both Christianity and Judaism. The cherubim were the only images in Solomon's Temple, and the ark was placed under the wings of the cherubim to symbolize the concentration of all natural life. They were the witnesses and representatives of God's glory. Angels appear in both Old and New Testaments.

Figure 1-9. A canvas work panel, 1 1/3 by 2 feet, depicting St. Michael as an angel, holding a sword in his right hand. Designed and executed by Bucky King. Photographed by W.S. King.

The Ten Commandments: The Ten Commandments were given to Moses on two tablets of stone. They are the foundation of belief for the Christian and Jewish faiths, often being referred to as the "tablets of the law," or "God's word." They may be represented in many ways, but are usually shown as Roman numerals on stone plates or as numbers in an open book or upon a scroll.

The Church: With the establishment of Christianity came the founding of the church and the erection of buildings quite different from synagogues. The building of these houses of worship came to represent the church itself. Other symbols used to represent the church are the ship and the beehive.

The Six-Pointed Star: This is a hexagram that consists of two equilateral triangles interlaced to form a star. It symbolizes God, the Creator, and is called "The Star of David," or "Magen David," in Hebrew. While many believe it to be a very old symbol, with origins dating back to antiquity, the symbol is actually fairly modern. It is currently used by Israel as its symbol, but the six-pointed star is universal. In Christianity it is a symbol for the Trinity, since the star is composed of two overlapping triangles.

The Ship: This is a symbol for Noah's ark and for the church as a whole body. Three ships are often used to represent the Trinity.

The Crown: This is a symbol for royalty—God's royalty in heaven and on earth—used by both Christians and Jews. When it is shown on top of the Tree of Life it represents the crown as the kingdom of God. When three crowns are used in Judaism, they symbolize the crown of the law, the priesthood, and royalty. Often the crown is used alone, featuring the Hebrew letters Kof and Tav, which are the initials of the words "Kesser Torah," or "Crown of the Torah."

15

PROPHETS, PATRIARCHS, AND GOSPELS

The narratives in the Old and New Testaments contain many stories and symbols. A few of these are Jonah and the whale, Noah's ark, the seven virgins, the loaves and the fish, Adam and Eve, The tree of Jesse, the saints, the gospelists—Matthew, Mark, Luke, and John—St. Paul, the twelve tribes of Israel, and the twelve disciples of Jesus.

There is a specific symbol for each of the disciples of Jesus and a specific symbol for St. Paul.

Symbols for Disciples and St. Paul

Disciple	*Symbol*
St. Peter—leader of the Apostles.	Crossed keys or an inverted cross, since he was crucified upside down.
St. Andrew—the Galilean fisherman.	A cross shaped as an X.
St. James—the Greater.	Three scallop shells, since he was a fisherman.
St. John—the Evangelist and fisherman.	A chalice with a serpent emerging.
St. Phillip—from Bethsaida.	The botonée flanked by round loaves of bread on the right and left, often with a cross in the center.
St. Bartholomew—martyred alive.	Three butcher's knives.
St. Thomas—doubting Thomas.	A spear and a carpenter's square.
St. Matthew—the tax collector.	Three money bags.
St. James, the Less—son of Alphaeus.	A saw or fuller club and sometimes three stones.
St. Jude—also known as Thaddeus.	A sailing ship.
St. Simon—the Zealot.	A fish and a book.
St. Matthias—chosen to replace Judas.	A double-edged axe and an open book.
Judas Iscariot—betrayer of Jesus.	A rope or a black square.
St. Paul—came after the twelve disciples.	A sword and an open book with the inscription, "spiritus gladius," or "sword of the spirit."

The symbols for the four Evangelists—Matthew, Mark, Luke, and John—are taken from the prophet Ezekial and the Revelation of St. John the Divine. They are generally referred to as the "Living Creatures."

Symbols for the Evangelists

Evangelist	Symbol
Matthew	The winged angel.
Mark	The winged lion.
Luke	The winged ox.
John	The winged eagle.

The twelve tribes of Israel have both a flag and a precious stone as their symbols.

Symbols for the Twelve Tribes of Israel

Tribe	Stone	Flag
Reuben	Ruby	Red flag with mandrakes.
Simeon	Smaragd	Green flag showing a picture of Schechem.
Levi	Carbuncle	Flag not known.
Judah	Emerald	Blue flag with lion.
Issachar	Sapphire	Black flag with the sun and moon.
Zebulum	White Pearl	White flag with a ship.
Dan	Topaz	Sapphire-colored flag with a snake.
Naphtali	Turquoise	Wine-red flag with an olive tree.
Gad	Crystal	Not known.
Asher	Chrysolite	Fire-red flag with an olive tree.
Joseph	Onyx	Black flag.
Benjamin	Jasper	Many-colored flag with a wolf.

ANIMALS AND PLANTS

The following is a list of animals and how they are used symbolically in religious art. Only a few are given here, since the list is quite lengthy.

Symbolic Use of Animals

Animal	*Symbolic Use*
Fish	In the early days of Christianity the followers of Jesus resorted to using secret signs to keep from exposing themselves to the foes of Christianity. The fish is used as a symbol for Christ because the Greek word for fish was used then to mean "Jesus Christ, Son of God, Savior." In modern times it has come to represent Jesus, the Savior.
Eagle	The symbol for St. John. Also, the eagle is a symbol of power in Judaism, since the eagle is the king of birds.
Peacock	Stands for resurrection, since it sheds its tail plumage but the plumage is brilliantly renewed.
Cock	Represents St. Peter's denial of Jesus.
Lamb	Symbolizes the "Angus Dies, the lamb of God," from St. John's Gospel, "Behold, the lamb of God, who takes away the sin of the world."
Ram	Symbolizes sacrifice, based on the Old Testament story of the sacrificial lamb.
Lion	The lion represents the power and courage of the tribe of Judah. When winged, the lion represents St. Mark.
Hart	A symbol for baptism, derived from the 42nd Psalm, "As the hart (bird) panteth after the water brooks, so panteth my soul after thee, oh God. My soul thirsteth for God, for the living God; when shall I come and appear before God?"
Pelican	This represents Christ and his atonement on the cross. The symbol stems from the fable that a pelican tears open her breast and feeds her young with her own lifeblood in times of famine.
Dove	Symbolizes peace and the people of Israel. In Christianity it represents the Holy Spirit, ascending and descending.

Plants have come to represent many symbols in both Christianity and Judaism because of the special characteristics of each plant or flower. The lily, for example, grows from a bulb and comes up again each year more beautiful than before, as does the annual feast of Easter. The lily of the valley is a humble plant, which is immuned to many pests. Each year it produces a pure white flower, delicately scented, which one has to examine carefully to appreciate; it becomes a natural symbol for purity and humility.

Symbolic Use of Plants

Plant	Symbolic Use
Vine (scroll)	In Christianity the vine is the reminder of Christ's words, "I am the vine, ye are the branches." In Judaism the vine represents the Jewish people as a whole, or the Tree of Life. Often in both religions the grapevine and wheat are used for symbols of the wine and bread.
Pomegranate	Symbolizes fertility of life for Jews and resurrection for Christians.
Palm	Symbolizes victory or Christ's ride into Jerusalem on the donkey. In the fifteenth century, it came to stand for martyrdom, since many saints were martyred, thus attaining victory.
Lily	Represents resurrection.
Rose	Stands for the Nativity and Christmas.
Lily of the Valley	Symbolizes purity and humility.
Passionflower	Represents Christ's sufferings.
Jesse Tree	Symbolizes Jesus' royal genealogy.
Mustard Seed	Stands for growth.

Figure 1-10. The fish is an important symbol in Christianity. This macrame fish is 3 feet long and features a driftwood fin and a chestnut bead eye. Designed and executed by Judy Elwood. Photographed by Ruth Carey.

LETTERS

The word calligraphy literally means handwriting. It comes from the Greek word, "callos," meaning beautiful and the Greek word "graphe," meaning writing. In other words calligraphy means to print, draw, write, or inscribe letters into a work of art. In religious art calligraphy itself is symbolic, since letters, initials, or phrases are used to convey ideas and thought. The manuscripts so handsomely illustrated in the Middle Ages by the monks of Europe show the extremes to which calligraphy can be used in order to enrich paintings and designs. Every page of these wonderful old books contains beautiful paintings and designs, which are enhanced by Greek or Latin script. The artist, Ben Shahn, has said, "Words and letters amplify and enrich the meaning of painting." Although less of us understand these languages, Hebrew, Greek, and Latin are still used. The major reason we continue to use them is that they can be universally understood by peoples of all tongues, thus uniting us with members of our faiths all over the world. During the last two decades the use of English in America to convey religious ideas through symbols has become increasingly popular. There is nothing wrong, for example, in using B and E for the "Beginning and the End," instead of the traditional Alpha and Omega. The phrase simply means that in the beginning when creation took place God was there, and he will be there at the end when the world and mankind cease to exist. This translates into any language. Since few of us today actually speak Greek, we can be equally devout and faithful in English, German, French, Spanish, or Italian.

Calligraphy is probably one of the most beautiful ways to use symbolic ideas, simply because it can be said in any language. All letters from any script or written language can be made into wonderful patterns of design on all sorts of surfaces. Robert Indiana is one artist who has already proven this with his marvelous rendering of the word "love." Over a million copies of his painting have been sold to date.

Popular Letter Symbols

The Tetragrammaton: This is used by both Christians and Jews. It is the quadrilateral name of God and is composed of the Hebrew letters Yod, Hay, Vov, and Hay, or YHWH, which is pronounced "Yahweh." The Jews have long been reluctant to utter the name of God, so over the centuries they developed other names. "Adonai" uses the two letter Yods. "Shaddai," meaning "the Almighty," is represented by the single letter Shin.

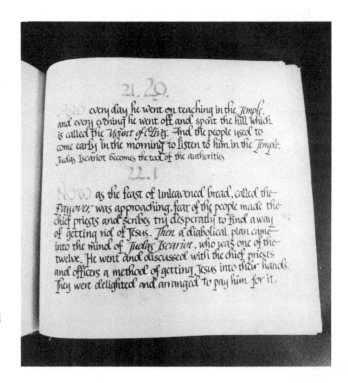

Figure 1-11. "The Gospel According to St. Luke." A page from a handmade book, calligraphed, illustrated, and bound by the artist. The book measures 12 by 12 by 3 inches. Designed and executed by William Hannon. Photographed by the artist.

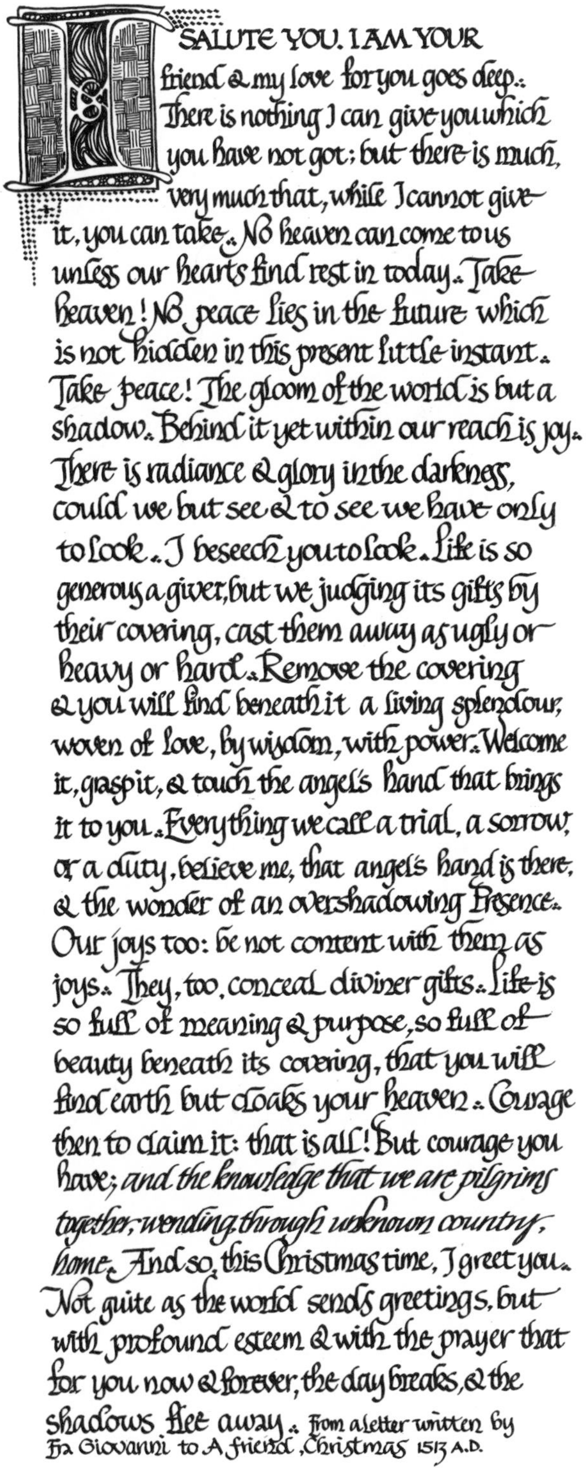

I SALUTE YOU. I AM YOUR friend & my love for you goes deep. There is nothing I can give you which you have not got; but there is much, very much that, while I cannot give it, you can take. No heaven can come to us unless our hearts find rest in today. Take heaven! No peace lies in the future which is not hidden in this present little instant. Take peace! The gloom of the world is but a shadow. Behind it yet within our reach is joy. There is radiance & glory in the darkness, could we but see & to see we have only to look. I beseech you to look. Life is so generous a giver, but we judging its gifts by their covering, cast them away as ugly or heavy or hard. Remove the covering & you will find beneath it a living splendour, woven of love, by wisdom, with power. Welcome it, grasp it, & touch the angel's hand that brings it to you. Everything we call a trial, a sorrow, or a duty, believe me, that angel's hand is there; & the wonder of an overshadowing Presence. Our joys too: be not content with them as joys. They, too, conceal diviner gifts. Life is so full of meaning & purpose, so full of beauty beneath its covering, that you will find earth but cloaks your heaven. Courage then to claim it: that is all! But courage you have; and the knowledge that we are pilgrims together, wending through unknown country, home. And so, this Christmas time, I greet you. Not quite as the world sends greetings, but with profound esteem & with the prayer that for you now & forever, the day breaks, & the shadows flee away. From a letter written by Fra Giovanni to a friend, Christmas 1513 A.D.

Figure 1-12. Calligraphy. The text is taken from a sixteenth-century letter. Designed and executed by William Hannon.

The Chi-Rho: This is the monogram of Jesus Christ. It stands for the P and X, which are the first two letters of the Greek word for Christ. The Chi-Rho has taken many forms and designs, which incorporate a cross or other letters. In later centuries the Chi-Rho was replaced by the initials IHC or IHS, which are the first three letters in the Greek word for Jesus. In the Greek alphabet the third letter in the word for Jesus is the uppercase form of our letter C; our English s is the lowercase form of that letter. Therefore, IHC and IHS mean the same thing.

Often a cross is flanked with the letters IC XC, which are the first and last letters of the Greek word for Jesus (IC) and Christ (XC). When this is followed by the inscription NIKA, it means "Jesus Christ, the Conqueror."

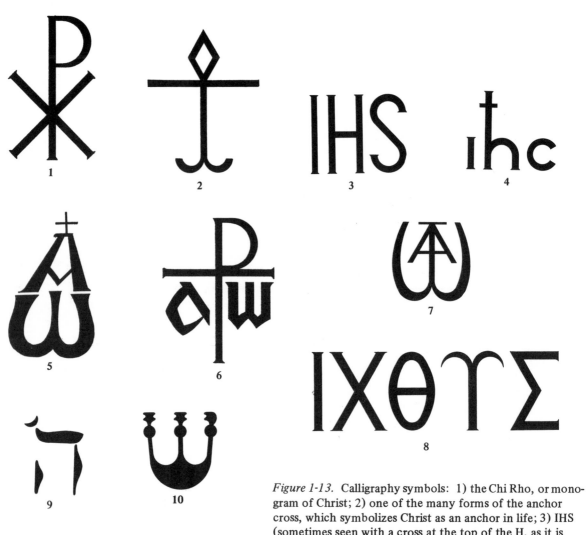

Figure 1-13. Calligraphy symbols: 1) the Chi Rho, or monogram of Christ; 2) one of the many forms of the anchor cross, which symbolizes Christ as an anchor in life; 3) IHS (sometimes seen with a cross at the top of the H, as it is shown here), which is a monogram for Christ, since it is the abbreviation of the Greek work for Jesus; 4) IHC, which is an earlier version of IHS monogram; 5) symbols for the Alpha and Omega — "the beginning and the end"; 6) the Chi Rho and the Alpha and Omega used together in one symbol to say that Christ was present at the beginning and he will be there at the end; 7) a contemporary version of the Alpha and Omega written as one symbol; 8) the Greek word for fish, the letters of which stand for "Jesus Christ, son of God, Savior"; 9) the single letter Ched with the letter Yod standing for "life"; 10) the Hebrew letter Shin (Augsburg script), standing for "Shaddai," meaning "the Almighty"; 11) a contemporary Shin.

Figure 1-14. This hanging, 30 by 39 feet, was done with the latch-hook rug technique and then mounted on a wooden frame. The colors, which were hand-dyed, are mustard, white, and a light royal blue. The central symbol is the Celtic cross, but other symbols are the Greek cross, the descending dove, the fish, the Maltese cross, the four-nailed cross, and the Alpha. Designed by Anne Driver Toumey. Executed by the Women's Circle for the Wexford Community Church, Wexford, Pennsylvania.

Figure 1-15. "The Suffering Servant." This appliqué wall hanging features letters that were cut out from hooked fabric. The letters spell out "Suffering Servant." Designed and executed by Nell Battle Booker Sonneman. Photographed by Darrel Acree.

23

CHAPTER 2.

ECCLESIASTICAL APPOINTMENTS

Both Christians and Jews use many articles in their public and private worship. The very nature of these articles allows the craftsman tremendous range in terms of method and technique. The following chart will give the craftsman some idea of the enormous range of objects there are to be made. It seems fitting to group them under general headings, rather than to separate them into categories by religion. The articles are arranged according to usage, regardless of whether they were executed in fiber, clay, wood, or metal. Some items appear under several headings—an indication that the article may be used in a number of ways.

Religious artwork should be highly original. It is neither possible, feasible, nor desirable to strive for uniformity; and, since size, color, and design vary so greatly, we have indicated an average size or specific rule only in some special cases. Needless to say, an artist need not be of a specific faith to create articles for that faith. His experience and desire to create is all that is needed.

FURNITURE

By furniture, we mean items used for specific purposes that usually remain in the house of worship permanently. They may be created from stone, wood, metal, clay, fiber, glass, plastic, or any material suited to the style of the building, the whims of the art committee, and the approval of the clergy. There are no specific size, color, or material requirements for any of these objects. The craftsman would be well advised to seek the opinion of the architect, however, in order to reach an understanding of the needs and desires of the congregation. Obviously, a huge baptismal font, for example, will not suit a small country church. Neither will tiny ark doors suit a large syngaogue. Although some contemporary works look quite handsome in antique buildings and settings, the artist must consider the desires of the congregation and clergy before executing any plan.

Since there are no specific rules regarding size in this area, we can only offer general hints.

Religious Art Objects

Furniture	Wall Decorations	Lighting	Vessels	Vesture	General Worship	Individual Worship
altars	stained	interior	ciboria	surplices	Torah mantels	jewelry
altar rails	glass	lights	patens	tallisim		crosses
baptismal	windows	exterior	wine cups	tallis bags	Torah	spice boxes
fonts	crosses	lights	Communion	tefillin	pointers	rosary beads
rugs	menorahs	menorahs	cups	bags	book bindings	rosary cases
kneelers	sculptures	Chanukah	water containers	chasubles		Nativity sets
alms basins	murals	lights	flower vases	stoles	Torah	Chanukah
benches	tapestries	eternal	chalices	maniples	binders	lights
pews	banners	lights	Seder cups	miters	altar frontals	menorahs
chairs	ark valances	chancel	Seder plates	copes		Seder cups
pulpits	ark	lights		morses	lecturn	Seder plates
lecturns	curtains	altar candlesticks		dalmatica	hangings	candlesticks
arks	dossals	Communion candlesticks		rings	pulpit falls	mezuzahs
ark doors	stations			jewelry	ark valances	challah
windows	of the					covers
ambrys	cross				ark curtains	matzoh
chuppahs	ambrys				funeral	covers
processional					palls	prayer
crosses					alms bags	books
altar					towels	Haggadahs
crosses					altar cloths	marriage certificates
					credence	birth certificates
					cloths	baptismal
					burses	forms
					veils	
					corporals	
					palls	
					purificators	

Altar: The altar is a table or solid block upon which the Holy Communion is consecrated during services. It is sometimes referred to as a "Communion table." It is also used in some denominations as a prayer table. In commercial catalogs an average altar runs 6 feet long by 3 feet wide, standing about 3¾ feet high. Few will meet this exact size, however, since they all vary as to function and use.

Altar rail: The rail or fence around, or directly in front of, the altar encloses the sanctuary surrounding the altar. It is used by the communicants to lean against when kneeling to receive Communion.

Baptismal font: The stand, pedestal, table, or device containing a basin for water used in the rite of baptism. It is very highly decorated and is usually placed in a special area of the house of worship. In specific denominations where the baptismal rite includes immersion, it may be of a size large enough to contain several persons.

Rugs and kneelers: Sizes of rugs and altar kneelers are predetermined by the existing furniture and appointments. Altar rail kneelers must fit the space allotted for them near the altar and beside the altar rail, while acolyte kneelers may be of varying size and design. Pew kneelers are usually leather or some hard-wearing upholstery cloth, but many churches in Europe have elegantly embroidered pew kneelers; no hard and fast rules apply here.

Figure 2-1. Altar rug and kneelers. The rug was worked in four separate sections and put together upon completion. The design incorporates stylized acanthus leaves and a Greek cross. The two kneelers shown depict the stories of Noah and the Loaves and the Fishes. All work was done in needlepoint and canvas work. Designed by Bucky King. Executed by Mrs. John Rankin and ladies of the congregation for the Lawrencefield Chapel in Wheeling, West Virginia. Photographed by Cress.

Altar rugs, placed in front of the altar or covering steps leading up to the altar, take their size and decoration from the existing appointments. All colors and symbols used should fit the general scheme of the building. Using a cross symbol in the design of the kneelers is frowned upon by some denominations.

Alms basin: This is usually a large plate of metal, in which are placed the alms and offerings of the congregation for presentation before the altar. These containers are handled a great deal and must bear the weight of both paper and coins. The craftsman should consider this carefully when planning the design and construction.

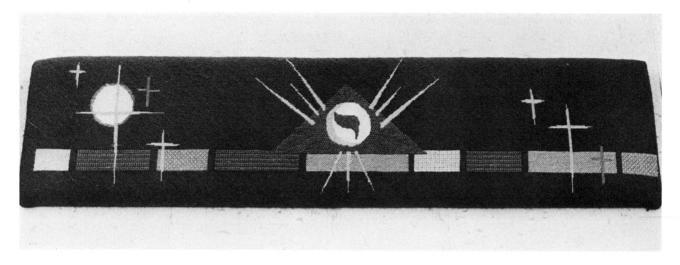

Figure 2-2a. One kneeler from a set of canvas work altar rail kneelers. Designed by Bucky King. Executed by Mrs. Graham Shaddick and other members of the Trinity Episcopal Church, Beaver, Pennsylvania. Photographed by Cress.

Figure 2-2b. A set of four kneelers, done in canvas work, representing the four Evangelists — Matthew, a human winged form; Mark, the winged lion; Luke, the winged ox; and John, the winged eagle. Designed by Bucky King. Executed by Mrs. Graham Shaddick and other members of the Trinity Episcopal Church, Beaver, Pennsylvania. Photographed by Cress.

27

Seating: Benches, pews, and chairs are used for seating and may be created in metal, wood, plastic, or any other suitable material. Carving and surface decoration may be used, and, if pew racks are used on the back of the pew to contain hymn books and Bibles, these may be of a different material. The size and arrangement of the seating is determined by the existing space.

Pulpit: This is a platform, usually elevated above the congregation, to the right or left side of the main chancel. It is equipped with a railing, steps and a reading desk, from which the sermon is preached. Wood, metal, and stone are generally the choices.

Lectern: The lectern is usually a stand, platform, or table placed to the right or left of the main chancel, from which the Scripture lessons are read. The material usually matches that of the pulpit, and the stand is often equipped with reading lights and a slanted top.

Ark: The ark contains the Torah and is centered in the middle area in the synagogue. Either curtains or doors are placed in front of the ark. The size of the ark is usually large enough to contain three or four Torahs or more, and it should be suited in design and proportion to the particular synagogue. Many materials are suitable, including stone, metal, wood, glass, plastic, and even leather. The doors, which face the congregation, may be of contrasting material, but must be arranged so that they open and close easily.

Windows: There are very few restrictions on windows, and stained glass is used to create decorations visible from both the inside and outside of the building. Placement is determined by the architect, though content of design may vary greatly. Windows may also be made of ceramic and plastic (to allow light to pass through), as well as many transparent acrylics set in metal or plastic frames. Windows in teaching rooms are often plain glass, and, although decoration may be used, it rarely is. The opportunity to decorate windows with contemporary materials such as plastics and ceramics is a huge new avenue for all craftsmen.

Ambry: This is a closed cupboard, wall hung or freestanding, situated close to the altar or in the sacristy for the preservation of the Eucharist, holy oils, and sacred vessels. Its size must be large enough to contain the vessels easily without crowding, but its decoration may be any that is suited to its function. Often the ambry is built right into the wall, but regardless, it may be of wood, metal, stone, ceramic, or other material.

Figure 2-3a. These ark doors and windows were made from Honduras mahogany and feature carvings representing the twelve-branch Tree of Life — one branch for each tribe of Israel. The richly colored stained glass panels placed on either side of the doors have rheostatically controlled illumination. Designed and executed by Joseph Perrin and Glynn Acree for the Helen E. Massell Chapel, Atlanta, Georgia under the council of Rabbi Rothschild.

Figure 2-3b. Ark doors open (see Figure 2-3a) revealing the inside of the ark and Torahs. Designed and executed by Joseph Perrin and Glynn Acree.

Chuppah: The wedding tent used in Jewish marriage services is a tentlike structure supported on four poles. Often a young man's wimple (Torah binder) is stretched between four poles to make the tent. There are practically no restrictions with respect to size, color, or design, and the chuppah is very often owned by the synagogue and used for all its wedding services.

Cross: The altar cross usually remains on the altar at all times, whereas the processional cross is placed on a pole and carried in front of a choir or ecclesiastical procession. The latter may be stored for these special uses in a specific place. If the figure of Christ is used upon the cross (crucifix), the figure must be in proportion to the overall size of the cross. In other words, a large cross does not warrant a tiny figure. Many materials are well suited for the cross motif, including wood, metal, stone, plastic, enamel, glass, and ivory.

WALL DECORATIONS

This category consists of decorative art objects that are installed permanently on the walls of a house of worship, including such things as stained glass, tapestries, murals, sculpture, ark doors, ark curtains, kappores (the valence over the ark doors), and even hanging menorahs. There is a large selection of possible materials and methods from which to choose, making consultation with the clergy, architect and congregation essential. Specific sizes, colors, and symbols must be selected to suit the physical setting and environment. Few restrictions are imposed by the denominations in this area.

Figure 2-4. "Hanging Menorah II." This 8 1/3- by 2-foot hanging menorah is essentially a tapestry hung from brass shapes. The brass shapes are in the form of the letter Shin (and its mirror image), which stands for the Almighty. The tapestry was woven in shades of green, olive, and gold. Designed and executed by Renate F. Chernoff. Courtesy of Heska Amuna Synagogue, Knoxville, Tennessee. Photographed by David E. Richer.

Figure 2-5. "Madonna and Child — after Raphael." Many different fabrics and several machine sewing techniques were incorporated to create this appliqué hanging done in homage to the painting by Raphael. The piece measures 3 square feet. Designed and executed by Margaret Cusak.

Figure 2-6. "Kings." This hooked wall hanging, measuring 3 by 5 feet, depicts the three kings present at the Nativity. The colors are reds, yellows, and oranges. Designed and executed by Judy Felgar. Photographed by Wayne Felgar.

Figure 2-7. "Corpus." A macrame figure of Christ hung from a simple wooden stick, forming a cross shape. Designed and executed by Douglas E. Fuchs.

33

Dossal: Many churches hang a dossal behind the altar, suited to the overall proportions of the altar. The dossal is either a neutral color or a color of the church season. Some large cathedrals have more than one dossal, changing them according to the church season. Dossals are beautifully decorated in woven techniques, tapestry, or stitchery. Fabric printing methods are also suitable.

Stations of the cross: In Roman Catholic churches, the stations of the cross are often wall hung. They consist of fourteen images, either representational or abstract, portraying the passion of Christ. A devotional service using these images may be said by individuals or by the congregation; special prayers and thoughts are said at each station. The stations may be created from fiber, clay, metal, glass, stone, ivory, wood, plastic, or any other suitable material. Their placement in the building should suit their use, and an allowance of at least 6 feet should be left in front of each station.

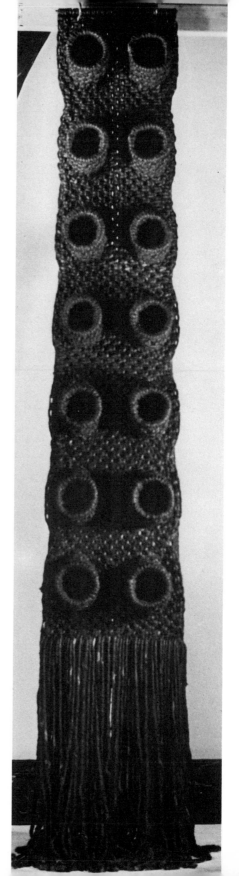

Figure 2-8. "Fourteen Stations of the Cross." This hanging, made with red jute and silver lamé threads is 11 by 2½ feet and ½ foot deep. Done with macrame and wrapping techniques, the piece symbolizes the stations that Christ walked through in Jerusalem on his way to Calvary. Designed and executed by Leora Klaymer Stewart.

LIGHTING

Of course, interior and exterior lighting must always be present, if only for the purpose of illumination in the building. Some lights are permanently installed, such as the menorah and eternal light, and some are used only for specific occasions, such as Communion candles or Chanukah lights.

Chanukah lights: These are eight-branch or nine-branch fixtures used for the Festival of Lights and the Feast of Rededication.

Eternal light: This is often used in both Christian and Jewish houses of worship. It is always left burning and is positioned in the main chancel area. The design may take many forms in varying materials. Eternal lights represent the light of God in the world.

Chancel light: This is used to illuminate the main building areas and is often purchased from commercial lighting houses to ensure uniformity when matched sets are desired. The design, color, and size is dictated by placement and use. However, ceramic craftspersons could easily find a large new area of design potential in this field.

Altar candlesticks: A variety of candleholders are used on altars and for specific services, such as Communions, weddings, funerals, and baptisms. For size, material, content, and design the clergy and art committee should be consulted. In new buildings there are often large memorial funds available for these objects.

Figure 2-9. This Trinity candle was made by waxing down, by color, used candles that were donated by members of the congregation. Using three one-gallon milk containers as molds, each color was shaped and then joined together to form this stylized candle. The stripes represent the diversity within the worshipping community. The candle stand is a wooden base with spiral macaroni glued onto it to form a design. It was later sprayed gold. Candle and stand measure 2 1/3 feet in height. Designed and executed by Ginnie and Ernie Wise for the lenten season observance at Trinity United Church of Christ, Tiffin, Ohio. Photographed by William Paul.

VESSELS

Some vessels and containers are used on specific occasions and some are permanently situated in churches and synagogues. The size, color, and decoration should be determined by their function. That is to say, if the congregation numbers over fifty, a chalice of suitable size is needed for Communion services. One that holds just eight ounces of consecrated wine would not do. On a large altar small flower vases would look ridiculous, so suitably sized vases are needed. The number of people served by either the vessel or container must be considered in their design.

Communion vessels: These include all containers used in the Eucharist services, such as wine cups, chalices, ciboria, patens, wine and water containers, and individual Communion cups, which are used to dispense the consecrated elements of bread and wine. The Communion service is the means by which the priest or clergy consecrates these elements. The symbols of bread and wine represent the sacred symbols of body and blood, which stand for Christ's death and passion.

Flower vase: Vases offer the widest range in design and material construction. They are used in nearly all services and for special services, such as weddings, funerals, and holidays. Because of the diversity of flower arrangements, nearly every house of worship desires a large selection of these containers to suit the arranged material. Many materials may be used, including gold and silver; form, shape, size, and decoration suitable for special religious feasts provide a very large range of ideas for craftsmen. Memorial funds are usually available for these containers.

Seder vessels: The Seder cup and plate, used in the Seder service during Passover, contain the wine and unleavened bread used symbolically in the service. A wide range of design in many materials is possible, and, since these are often presented as gifts, they constitute a major area for consideration.

Eucharistic vessels: The chalice (wine cup), paten (bread or wafer plate, which sits on top of the chalice), and the ciborium (bread box, which holds the unconsecrated bread before the Communion service) are usually made of gold or silver—the most precious metals—though other materials may be used. Their design should suit their function. Chalice heights range from 10 to 15 inches with a cup diameter of 6 to 8 inches. The paten sits on top of the chalice; its bottom rim must fit securely into the top of the chalice. The ciborium contains the bread before it is consecrated in the Eucharist service, so its size is controlled by the number of wafers it must hold at maximum capacity.

VESTURE

The term vesture includes all items that are worn during services by a priest, minister, rabbi, or other clergyman, including items of jewelry. Choir robes, or cottas, fall under this category, but are usually ordered from commercial firms as an economy measure. Many are needed in different sizes, and it is one item that can usually be furnished more reasonably by commercial houses.

Surplice: This is the outer vestment worn by Roman and Anglican Catholic clergymen of various offices. It is of white, flowing fabric with wide open sleeves that usually hang below the knee. Surplices have been commercially made for many years and, unless specific embroidery or surface decoration is desired, they can be ordered more reasonably from commercial houses.

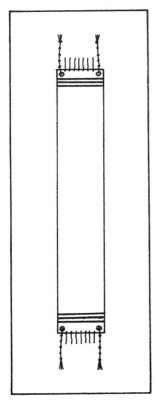

Figure 2-10. Straight rectangular tallis.

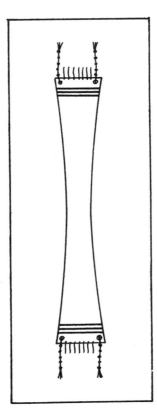

Figure 2-11. Shaped tallis, narrowing at neck.

Tallis: The tallis, or prayer shawl, is usually 1½ feet wide by at least 6 feet long, depending on the height of the rabbi or owner. It is edged with fringe and four corner fringes, which are called "zizis." These should be wrapped and knotted by hand in a prescribed manner (See *Embroideries and Fabrics for the Synagogue and Home* listed in the "Bibliography.") Any fabric that drapes well is suitable for this purpose, but mixtures of wool and linen in the fiber content are forbidden among the Orthodox Jews. A tallis may be all wool, all linen, or a combination of synthetic fibers, perhaps mixed with linen, cotton, or wool. Also, very heavy fabrics or tapestries are not suitable because they are apt to be too warm for indoor use. The tallis may be decorated with stripes, lettering, and designs in appliqué, embroidery or many other fiber techniques. The tallis bag (for carrying the tallis) may be of any fiber and decoration. Many prayer shawls are now tapered and shaped at the neck, no longer conforming to the pure rectangular form.

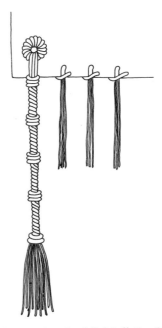

Figure 2-12. Enlarged sketch of "zizis," the four corner fringes.

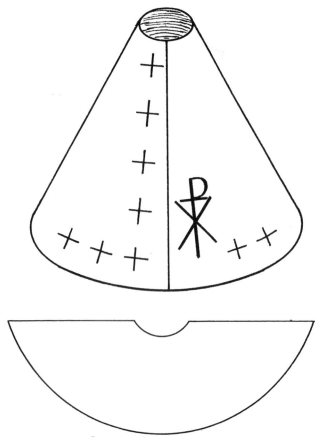

Figure 2-13. Conical chasuble and its pattern.

Tefillin bag: The bag which contains the phylacteries may be of any size and any material adorned with any type of decoration. Phylacteries are small black boxes that contain sacred inscriptions. They are approximately the width of two fingers and are worn on the arm and forehead of Jewish men during prayers, either at home or in the synagogue.

Eucharistic vesture: The chasuble, stole, and maniple, worn by the priest during mass or Holy Communion, follow the liturgical colors of the church year—red, green, white, purple, and sometimes blue. The fabric shoud drape well, but other than that requirement, design possibilities are limitless. Stoles and chasubles are usually made from the same cloth to match as a set. The chasuble can be made in several different styles according to the priest's personal taste. There are two kinds of stoles. The Eucharistic stole is usually 9 feet long by 3½ inches wide. It is seamed at the neck with a cross, which is required by Roman Catholics. Fringes at the ends of the stoles are not strictly required; their origin is derived directly from the fringes of the tallis. The

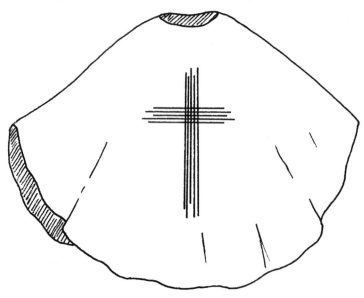

Figure 2-14. Gothic chasuble.

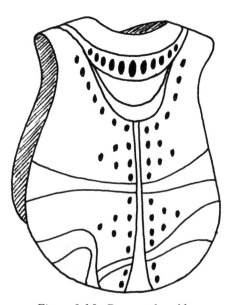

Figure 2-15. Roman chasuble.

Figure 2-16. Cope with soft hood.

maniple should match the stole and is usually 4 feet long (before folding) by 2½ inches wide. A wide choice of decoration may be used on all these vestments.

Cope and miter: The cope and miter (hat) are garments worn by a bishop. Copes are semicircular in shape with a wide border (orphrey) running from the neck to the floor. The average length down the center back seam is 5 feet and the straight edge of the semicircle averages 124 to 130 inches. A hood is optional. The orphrey averages 4 to 6 inches in width. If richly decorated, the body of the cope should be more restrained, and vice versa. A morse, or clasp, is used to hold the cope together below the neck. It buttons the vestment on the wearer and helps to hold it in place around the shoulders. The morse is usually made of gold, silver, or a precious metal, richly decorated, but it may also be embroidered. The colors of the cope and miter usually match, but they do not need to conform to the colors of the church year. Size is determined by the wearer.

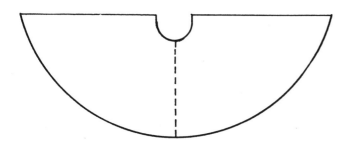

Figure 2-17. Semicircular pattern for cope.

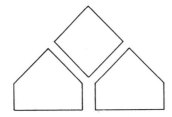

Figure 2-18. Pattern for miter.

Figure 2-19. Miter.

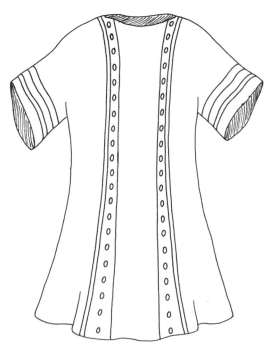

Figure 2-20. Pattern for dalmatic.

Figure 2-21. Front side of dalmatic, showing the bands plus an apparel below the neck.

Dalmatic: The tunicle, or dalmatic, is worn by the deacon or subdeacon without the chasuble. It is also worn by the priest sometimes under the chasuble. Although there are no specific color requirements, the dalmatic is made of lightweight fabric, usually white. This garment forms part of the full set of Eucharistic vestments (chasuble, stole, maniple, and dalmatic) used in high services of the Roman and Anglican Catholic churches. It has two bands (clavi) that run from shoulder to hem, in the front and in the back, which are often supplemented by a panel (apparel) across the center toward the neck.

Jewelry: Rings and neck chains bearing crosses are often worn by the clergy. Bishops often wear a bishop's ring, which may also bear the shield of the local diocese. The design, material content, and decoration of these items is personal; each clergy member will desire different styles and techniques.

ARTICLES USED IN GENERAL WORSHIP

All items under this heading are used in general or specific worship and are not necessarily on permanent view within the building.

Torah mantel: Mantels vary in size according to the actual size of the Torah, so it is essential that the craftsman know the exact size in order to produce a covering that fits properly. Fiber, metal, wood, or leather are all suitable materials. The color is optional, but white is usually used for the High Holy Days (Rosh Hashanah and Yom Kippur). When mounting them, holes must be left in the top for the Torah roller poles. The Torah is a scroll, hand-lettered, containing the five books of Moses, beginning with Genesis and ending with Deuteronomy. The covering used upon it is called the Torah mantel and is always richly decorated, woven, or printed in the finest materials.

Figure 2-22. Three Torah mantels. The mantel on the left represents the burning bush, from which God spoke to Moses. The letter Shin, symbolizing "the Almighty," is in the center. The center mantel depicts the seven pillars of the first Temple and draws attention to the silver crown on top of the Torah. The mantel on the right depicts a crown incorporating the letters for "Kesser Torah," which means "crown of the Torah." All three mantels were done with metal-thread embroidery techniques — the two on each end in gold, the one in the middle in silver. Designed and executed by Dorothy E. Wolken, a former student of Bucky King's, and given as a memorial to the Temple Israel in Canton, Ohio.

Torah pointer: The pointer, used to follow the script on the Torah, is usually 1 to 1½ feet long and may be made of wood, metal, enamel, or precious stone. Many feature a small hand carved at the end with its forefinger extended.

Book bindings: Book bindings for prayer books and Bibles vary greatly in size, but many different materials are suitable for use. Leather, embroidery, tapestry, enamel, silver or gold, or even wood and metal inlays are all possibilities.

Torah binder: Binders for the Torah are often called "wimples," or "wrappers," and come in two distinct styles. The wimple, which is the oldest style, is a very long strip of fabric, 8 to 10 inches wide and up to 10 feet in length. Here a great variety of decoration is possible, either woven, embroidered, or carefully batiked or printed. Wrappers are more modern binders. They are quite narrow strips of fabric, 3 to 5 inches wide, fastened by an elaborate clasp that secures them tightly around the Torah. The decoration is often specified by the donor, leaving the craftsman little choice. However, Torah binders wear out frequently; craftsmen interested in this area should make up samples suitable for presentation.

Altar frontals, lectern hangings, pulpit falls: Altar frontals, lectern hangings, and pulpit falls (hangings) are usually made in sets using colors of the church year. Many demoninations own sets of green, white, purple, and red for each of the seasons. These sets are frequent memorial donations. The altar frontal is a decorative covering, hanging directly in front of the altar. The lectern and pulpit hangings are suspended from pedestals. Their size depends exclusively on the size of the altar, pulpit, and lectern from which they hang. There is no fabric restriction, but the decoration should suit the season of the church year. Decoration with metal–thread embroidery, so often done in poor taste, is not a requirement, but has come to be expected through common use. Actually, any fiber technique is acceptable, including weaving, batik, printing, embroidery, macrame, and lace.

Figure 2-23a. Part of an appliquéd altar frontal done in three parts. This part is entitled "Resurrection: The Tree of Life." The area shown here measures 3¼ feet by 5 feet wide and is placed in front of the altar. Designed and executed by Nell Battle Booker Sonneman for the Shrine of the Blessed Sacrament, Washington, D.C.

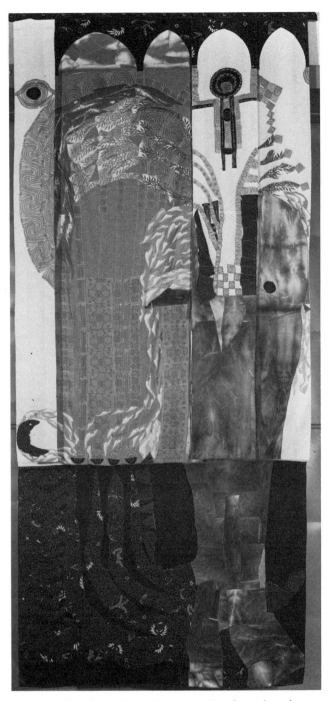

Figure 2-23b. Part of the three-part altar frontal set (see Figures 2-23a and c). This piece goes on the left side of the main altar and is entitled "Resurrection: The Phoenix."

Figure 2-23c. The third part of the three-piece altar frontal (see Figures 2-23a and b). This part belongs on the right side of the main alter. It is entitled "Resurrection: The Sign of Jonah" and measures 9 2/3 feet high and 4 1/6 feet wide.

Ark curtains: Ark curtains and the matching valances (kappores) if used, have no color or fabric requirements. The size is determined by the size of the ark. They must be fitted to operate easily, since they are opened and closed frequently.

Funeral pall: A funeral pall is a large casket cover made to fit the average size casket. There is no liturgical color or decoration requirement, but fabric used should drape well. Lead weights are often used in the four corners to keep the pall in position and to prevent slipping when the casket is moved.

Alms bags: Alms bags are used by some churches in place of the more conventional basins. The bags are attached to a long pole for passing among the pews. Heavy fabric is most suitable and there is no decorative restriction. Alms bags provide a somewhat quieter method of securing the annual Sunday collection than the usual metal basins.

Towels: Lavabo and baptismal towels are usually white linen, ranging in size from 10 to 12 inches wide by 18 to 24 inches long. Decoration is optional, but it should be kept in mind when the fabric is being chosen that they must be washed frequently.

Altar cloth: The altar cloth is often referred to as the "fair linen." It is made to fit the altar, hanging almost to the floor on both ends. Usually made of white linen, the ends may be decorated in any fashion. Some denominations, however, require that there be five small crosses, one at each corner of the altar top and one in the center front of the altar top. Often there is a matching credence cloth to cover the credence table or shelf where the Eucharistic vessels are placed. Both articles should be hand-hemmed. Crosses are not required on the credence cloth.

Burse and veil: The burse and veil cover the chalice, paten, and pall when they are placed upon the altar before the Communion service. The usual order is to place the chalice upon the corporal, which is centered in the middle of the altar cloth. The paten rests on top of the chalice, and the whole compacted unit is covered by the pall, which supports the veil. On top of the veil rests the matching burse. The burse is made in a square shape, hinged at the side much like a book. It opens to contain the purificators, which are used to wipe the chalice rim, sometimes an extra chalice veil, and the corporal. If an extra linen chalice veil is contained, it is usually white, not matching the liturgical colors used on the burse and chalice veil, and of a fine gauzelike quality. The burse is usually 8 to 10 inches square, stiffened to retain its shape with thin plastic or heavy cardboard. There are no fabric or decoration restrictions for either the burse or veil, although the decoration on the veil is often placed only on the side facing the congregation. Both articles are always the appropriate liturgical color for the church year. The veil covers the compacted chalice, paten, and pall, the size being determined by the height of the chalice, ranging from 1½ to 2 feet square. The decoration for both articles should be compatible because they are always used together.

Corporal: The corporal is usually made of white linen, hand-hemmed, and folded into threes to fit inside the burse. It can be 1½ to 2 feet square after hemming and is placed in the center of the altar upon the altar cloth. The chalice rests upon it. A cross is usually worked in the center front area. Since it must be washed and ironed frequently, however, surface decoration should be restrained. Roman Catholicism requires that a cross appear in the center front section.

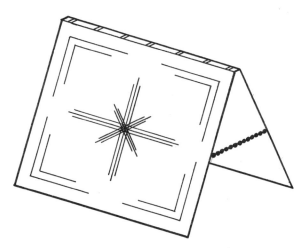

Figure 2-24. Burse standing up and open.

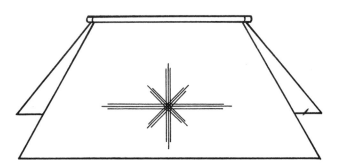

Figure 2-25. Burse resting on top of a veil, supported by a chalice and pall.

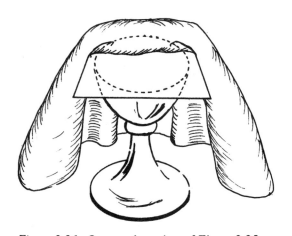

Figure 2-26. Open end-up view of Figure 2-25.

Pall: The pall is a thin square of plastic, covered with fine linen, that rests upon the paten and supports the chalice veil. It is usually not decorated.

Purificator: A small linen wiping cloth is called a purificator. It is usually made of fine white linen, hand-hemmed, and folded into threes. Since purificators are used to clean the rim of the chalice, they must be washed frequently. They are kept inside the burse until they are needed to wipe and dry the Communion vessels. The range in size is from 9 to 12 inches square. Linen is the most suitable fabric, due to the frequent washing, ironing, and often bleaching required. A small cross is usually hand-embroidered in the center.

ARTICLES USED IN PRIVATE WORSHIP

Some of these items are also used in general services, but a great deal more freedom can be exercised in the decoration and certainly a far wider range of materials and methods can be used when making the object for private use. All craftsmen interested in this area should keep samples of their work on hand. Many can find very profitable outlets in church and synagogue liturgical shops.

Jewelry: All manner of crosses, symbols, amulets, and religious designs can be created in wood, metal, stone, enamel, fiber, and ceramics. Spice boxes, rosary cases, rosary beads, and crosses are far too often mass-produced. Originals in any size and color would be a welcome addition to church and synagogue shops. Many personal items such as Nativity sets, Chanukah lights, Seder cups and plates, and all types of candlesticks offer the craftsman a wide range of selection, since no specific method, material, or technique is required. Usually, the Christmas season brings these articles out at various craft shows and sales, but they can be sold all year round.

Mezuzah: The mezuzah is an amulet placed on the doorpost of many Jewish homes as a symbol of good luck. It usually contains a tiny parchment scroll bearing passages from the Bible and the Hebrew letter Shin. Many materials, such as wood, enamel, ceramics, metal, plastic, and bone, are suitable.

Figure 2-27. A cast sterling silver mezuzah, approximately 3 inches tall and 3/4 inches wide. Designed and executed by Renate F. Chernoff. Courtesy of Mr. and Mrs. Sam Sayah. Photographed by David E. Richer.

Challah and matzoh covers: Items such as challah and matzoh covers are too often mass-produced, and more creative thought and design in this area is greatly needed. The challah cover is made from a fabric suitable for covering the Sabbath or festival bread; the matzoh cover is similar, covering the unleavened bread during the Passover holiday. Both may have suitable scripture embroidered upon them, or batiked, or even silk-screened.

Book bindings: Personal book bindings for Bibles, prayer books, and Haggadahs (prayer books for the Passover Seder) may include the initials or name of the owner. Calligraphy on marriage certificates or birth and baptismal forms may be specially designed. Bindings may be in various materials—fabric, tapestry, leather, metal, or wood. Some calligraphers may care to investigate this area more closely with the idea in mind of specializing in this field.

FIBER, CLAY, METAL, AND WOOD

Many craftsmen work in a variety of mediums, some doing both ceramics and textiles or some engaged in metal and wood. Though tradition has come to focus attention on certain materials for specific purposes, there is usually no hard and fast rule. The new plastics and metal compounds together with a great variety of synthetics offer a whole new world for the creative person. The heavy use of metal-thread embroidery during the early part of this century does not mean it is a binding requirement. The appeal of the material used will be determined by the expertise displayed by the craftsman. In order to give a better idea of the traditional materials used for religious articles mentioned in this chapter, we offer this chart. It is only a suggestion, however, of some of the possibilities.

Traditional Materials Used for Religious Articles

Judaism	Christianity
Metal, Stone, Wood, or Enamel	
ark doors	alms basins
pulpits	candlesticks
ark lights	crosses
Torah mantels	ciboria
Torah pointers	wine and water vessels
Torah tops	chalices
book bindings	patens
eternal lights	altars
lecturns	pulpits
chairs	pews
benches	chairs
menorahs	lecturns
vases	eternal lights
Seder cups	kneeling benches
Seder plates	book bindings
Chanukah lights	vases
lighting	ambrys
	baptismal fonts
	morses
	lighting
Fiber	
ark curtains	altar frontals
ark valances	fair linens
Torah mantels	funeral palls
book bindings	book bindings
wedding tents	kneelers
wimpels and wrappers	rugs
lecturn covers	alms bags
challah covers	surplices
matzoh covers	stoles
tallisim	burses
tallis bags	veils
tefillin bags	pulpit and lecturn hangings
wall hangings	chasubles
chair covers	dalmatics
bench covers	dossals

Judaism	Christianity
Fiber	
yarmulkes	maniples
	copes
	miters
	corporals
	palls
	purificators
	towels
Glass, Clay, or Enamel	
windows	windows
eternal lights	doors
doors	eternal lights
menorahs	private communion services
Chanukah lights	lighting
lighting	murals
murals	ambrys
Seder cups	crosses
Seder plates	
Leather	
book bindings	book bindings
chair coverings	kneelers
bench covers	chair covers
tallis bags	bench covers
tefillin bags	hangings
hangings	
Plastic	
windows	windows
ark doors	crosses
Torah mantels	book bindings
Torah pointers	candlesticks
book bindings	stations of the cross
Chanukah lights	Nativity sets
Seder cups	seating
Seder plates	banners
spice boxes	
mezuzahs	
amulets	

CHAPTER 3.

THE CLERGY AND THE CRAFTSMAN – FINDING THE CRAFTSMAN FOR THE JOB

For many centuries it was the habit of the popes to collect religious art. Urban VIII commissioned Bernini to transform the face of Rome. The results, seen in galleries and museums around the world, culminated in Raphael's and Michelangelo's great achievements. This lofty tradition, still seen in such great European cathedrals as Westminster Abbey, has unfortunately ebbed away. There have been some bouts of revival in church patronage of the arts with Matisse's chapel at Vence and Corbusier's at Ronchamp. But, for the most part, church patronage of the arts and crafts has declined steadily in America. England alone has seen fit to foster a revival through the efforts of great architects and men like Graham Sutherland.

The friendship, partnership, and communion that has always existed between the church/synagogue and the artist/craftsman should be re-established. Part of the problem in America rests with the fact that clergymen and congregations have found it easier and cheaper to purchase their merchandise from commercial religious-supply catalogs, rather than to seek out the qualified artisan. Congregations receive millions of tax free dollars yearly for the maintenance and management of their individual houses of worship. The total receipts of five of the leading denominations combined is well over twenty million dollars. If only ten percent of this were allocated for handcrafted, as opposed to catalog-purchased, merchandise, there would be two million dollars available for the crafts community. Think what a boost this would be for the craftsmen, and think what a spiritual boost it would provide for the congregations to have original, handcrafted items adorning their houses of worship.

A large portion of each denomination's yearly capital intake is given specifically in the form of memorials, very often designating individual items. Yet, the control groups rarely bother to solicit, advertise, or otherwise make known to the artist/craftsman their needs and requirements. They have at hand three to five catalogs of mass-produced ecclesiastical crafts from which to choose. Neither do the catalog houses offer to represent the individual craftsman who wishes to create unique originals only. Evidently, they feel that the time and expense involved would not justify the results. A study of 147 individual craftsmen revealed that Jewish and Episcopal congregations patronize the arts more than other congregations. Unitarians and Lutherans run second. But all congregations need to patronize the arts more than they are doing at present.

The religious-supply houses are not to be blamed for the existing situation. They have had years to watch it grow and develop and have simply capitalized on it by increasing their color illustrations and products offered. After all, they are in business to make a profit and they are entitled to make it. Education of the clergy and the control bodies of each congregation is essential if craftsmen and artists are to re-establish a friendship with the religious community mutually beneficial to both. This void between clergy and the artist/craftsman has been evident in the last fifty years or so in religion's embarassing inability to provoke aesthetic responses from the art community. The doors at both ends need to be opened widely. The religious control bodies must come to feel an obligation to the artisan to provide equal opportunity. Given a fair chance most artists/craftsmen will compete fairly with catalog prices. Furthermore, they can guarantee that the work created will be original and not mass-produced.

Once the congregation or clergyman has decided to secure specific work or to remodel the sanctuary, they have taken the first step. Not all clergymen are well versed or sympathetic toward the arts, so it is very helpful if the congregation establishes an art committee which will make all decisions, including funds and media. Funds are usually obtained directly through memorials, which are often for specific bequests, and from donations.

The first consideration should be the congregation. There may well be craftsmen immediately available with the right background and experience. For those who have the qualifications but have never attempted specific liturgical designs, the bib-liography included at the end of the book should be encouraging. Both the survey and how-to books will provide technical and design ideas. Amateurs within the congregation should be urged to help the professional craftsman with the technical work. Making a community project out of it personalizes the approach and gives members of the congregation an opportunity to help.

Perhaps there are talented embroiderers, woodcarvers, and glassblowers in the congregation who have the technical ability, but no talent for designing. The local art museum or craft guild should be consulted. They often keep lists of people with individual talents. Art centers and guilds usually are aware of the local material suppliers that would deal fairly with tax exempt bodies. The congregation should not expect discounts, however, from every supplier simply because the house of worship is a nonprofit organization. They should seek out those business people in the congregation who might be able to assist in arranging favorable discounts. Local colleges and universities may also be of great help, since professional craftsmen employed in the art departments are happy to take on consultant work.

Local art centers, guilds, and craft shops can also supply a list of craft fairs. When it is possible and feasible, attending these fairs provides direct contact with the artisans and their work. Seeing the actual work helps to provide an overall feeling for their techniques and price range.

Advertising the needs and requirements on a simple xeroxed flyer, which can be posted in craft shops, colleges, universities, museums, art centers, and craft guilds, offers the best chance for success. The flyer should include specific requirements essential so that the congregation won't be swamped with replies. Included on the flyer should be size—either specific or approximate—color suggestions or requirements, material to be used—fiber, clay, metal, wood, etc.—and desired technique. The craftsmen replying to such a flyer should supply slides or photos of past work, sketches or drawings of proposed work, and an estimate of costs and time needed to complete the work. The committee should arrange for the craftsman to actually see the setting and environment for the proposed work before expecting any submission from him. A discussion of approximate funds available and any specific details should take place at this time.

Liturgical commissions require a great deal of tact and understanding on the part of both parties. If the committee expects to pay the craftsman over a period of months, this should be stated plainly. Members of the art committee should remember that in interviewing the craftsman, they are seeking professionalism in design and technique; the craftsman may have well-founded reasons for disagreeing with the plans.

When the craftsman's designs and procedures have been agreed upon it is wise to draw up a contract, stating exactly what is required and the time limit for production. Since the item in question has not been seen at this time, a clause should be inserted in the contract that enables the art committee to reject the item if it varies greatly from the stated descriptions, sketches, or examples or if it is faulty in some way.

Last but not least, no matter how good a craftsman's portfolio is, there is nothing more graphic than an enthusiastic recommendation from a satisfied customer. If the congregation is satisfied with the work, hopefully they will say so.

CHAPTER 4.

THE CRAFTSMAN AND THE CLERGY – OPPORTUNITIES FOR THE CRAFTSMAN

Many craftsmen throughout the country are involved in domestic crafts. They are either production craftsmen or specialists who work only on commission. Hundreds have avoided liturgical commissions, feeling that to design for specific requirements is too tedious or creatively confining. Some feel they must reduce their fees because the work is for a house of worship, and others have experienced difficulty in being paid. Craftsmen have to earn a living, just as butchers, bakers, and mechanics do, and are entitled to fair fees for their work and services. They are sometimes overlooked for liturgical work because the worshipping body has used the services of commercial liturgical-supply houses, without ever investigating the local craft situation. But the field of ecclesiastical crafts widens daily and there is an increasing need for original work. Every congregation should be a source of infinite possibilities for the artist/craftsman.

A certain percentage of all craftsmen (roughly forty percent) are production craftsmen, who make similar, but not completely identical, work.

These people are weavers, potters, silversmiths, sculptors, wood-carvers, and glassworkers for the major part. They are accustomed to producing many items of a similar nature, but should perhaps start to consider making unique pieces, whose character could not be changed by copies. Their fear that some ecclesiastical items are too confining, could be lessened were they to be reminded that abstract forms are often acceptable in modern churches and synagogues. It helps to learn a few basic principles that can be applied to several denominations, such as appropriate colors or a few symbols that can be used in different ways.

It is the habit of many congregations to sell religious jewelry and other small liturgical items after services or at bazaars and festivals in order to make money for a Sunday school program or other cause. Since a percentage is retained by the church or synagogue anyway, there is no reason why local craftsmen could not avail themselves of this excellent opportunity; they face the same percentage mark-up in shops and galleries, anyway.

Although it is not the present practice of craft fairs to have liturgical booths, there is no reason why this could not be started. Even one booth allowing craftsmen in all areas of fiber, clay, metal, wood, and glass to exhibit would be a step forward. There are too few religious craft exhibitions held yearly, and it seems a worthy idea to include liturgical crafts as a special category in many of the craft shows held all over the country.

Many craftsmen work only on commission, because the nature of their work either requires a considerable cash outlay or because they work best under a given set of specifications. It is essential for these people to keep up-to-date portfolios including slides, photographs, references, and material costs. There is no substitute for a fine display portfolio and samples of materials.

Once the commission has been received the craftsman should maintain an attitude of giving and compromise. He should allow time to spare when questions arise or changes need to be made. When the committee's ideas conflict with his, he should make suggestions and give reasons to support his own thinking without being egotistical. In working out a time schedule for completion of work, he must allow himself some leeway for illness, injury, or other such problems that do arise from time to time.

Printing up a flyer of his work and services, illustrated with a few good photos and some reference quotes, will pay for itself in the work it brings. It is also a ready form of advertising to mail to new churches and synagogues and is useful at craft fairs and as hand-out material.

In many instances the congregation will feel that the actual work can be accomplished by members of their own congregation and that all they require are the paid services of a professional consultant. This is especially true of fiber projects, such as kneelers, banners, hangings, and rugs, but it can also apply to mosaics, plaques, and stained glass.

Usually, the consultant is also the designer. Overseeing a project from beginning to end can be a very rewarding goal. Consultants are usually responsible for the design, the production of the work, management of the workers, material purchasing and disbursement, handling of the work in progress, and installation. Occasionally, his responsibilities will include giving workshops and slide lectures. An overall fee is usually charged by the craftsman, depending on the amount of time involved and the extent of meeting time required with the workers.

For the craftsman who wishes to submit religious-oriented work, but is unaware of the procedures, we offer these guidelines.

Portfolio: The portfolio should include photos, slides, and illustrations of the work. Newspaper clippings and references are also very helpful. His professional background, shows and exhibitions in which he has participated, and any prizes he may have won are a must. It is also a good idea for him to have material costs readily available and to be able to present these in a competitive way. Actual samples of materials are very helpful too.

Interview: The craftsman should discuss the ideas of the committee or clergy fully, so that he understands them thoroughly before submitting. He should ask for any specific rules in the church or synagogue which will affect color, size, design, decoration, or function of the piece in question. When the clergy or committee is in doubt as to symbolism, he should be prepared to offer an alternative suggestion. The actual setting and environment in which the piece will eventually reside should be viewed so that he is familiar with surrounding colors, symbolism, and building decor. He should not give a rough estimate that he is going to have to change later. It is better for him to tell the truth and say that he must figure up the total costs, and that they will appear on his submission sheets.

Submission: The submission sheets should include the actual bid and all costs involved, together with drawings and sketches, either to actual size or to scale. Where feasible and practical, they should also include material samples, especially in the fiber field.

Contract: Many times it is advisable to have a signed contract for mutual protection of both parties, especially if many months will pass by before the completion of the work. Letters of intent will also suffice. The contract should state exactly what services or work will be rendered for the committee and congregation, the costs, and the time duration. There should be a clause inserted which will protect the church in case of default by the craftsman and vice versa.

The look of tomorrow's churches and synagogues will depend on the talents of the artist/craftsman, high standards, and his ability to get along with his fellow men.

CHAPTER 5.

CERAMICS IN ECCLESIASTICAL CRAFTS

Clay is a very pliable medium and allows for a full range of color and design ideas. It has been shaped and formed into all kinds of necessary containers by primitive cultures, as well as by modern man. Once fired it can withstand indoor and outdoor environments even in adverse climates. Although it will shatter under excessive pressure, with normal care many fine antique pieces have survived several centuries. Many of the Oriental porcelains of bygone days are still visible in museums, proving its durable qualities. Unlike metal, it is relatively inexpensive as a base material and takes its exquisite form and colors from the hands that shape it into objects.

History has shown us the many ways clay was used in previous centuries. Certainly, it was present in biblical times as water jugs, vases, cups, oil lamps, and candleholders. The Byzantine mosaics of the fourth through eighth centuries indicate how it was used in those times to create wall and floor murals, and certainly it reached a supreme high in the ever-present vase of Rome in the first century A.D. The floor and wall tiles in southern Spain tell us of the Moorish influence left behind. In fact, all types and styles of clay ornaments, vases, jugs, and sculptured gods keep appearing in the archaeologists' continued search for new evidence of early cultures. The fact that it can be poured, as well as worked in a lump state, has caused its rise from humble beginnings to the dinner service of kings, where it has graced many a table as fine porcelain. Many of the great synagogues and churches of Europe are decorated with clay mosaics and murals depicting religious events or stories, and it would be impossible to estimate how many clay lamps or candleholders have burned for religious purposes. Clay can be rendered into a very beautiful state by the hands that mold and shape it, as history only too well informs us.

Today our modern ceramic craftsmen have only scratched the surface of its possible use in religious art. There is a vast opportunity here for both the individual potter and the production potter. A few suggestions for contemporary ideas are perhaps needed to give them a head start.

Figure 5-1. "Everlasting Light." The durable properties of porcelain are beautifully put to use in this 2- by 2-foot abstract menorah. Designed and executed by David F. Silverman. Photographed by the artist.

Figure 5-2. "Crown of Thorns." This stoneware clay cylinder and bowl form one piece, as shown here, or can be used as two pieces. Designed for the lenten season, it features a crown of thorns pattern on the bowl and a dark plum matte glaze. The height of the cylinder is 2½ feet. Designed and executed by Sue Barnes. Courtesy of the Belle Meade United Methodist Church, Nashville, Tennessee. Flower arrangement by Jack Inman. Photographed by Lucille Sterling.

Figure 5-3. Chalice, paten, and water and wine containers
in ceramic. Designed and executed by Nancy and George
Wettlaufer.

Figure 5-5. "St. Francis of Assisi." This 14-inch stoneware figure, finished in reddish brown, was made using the coil method of construction. Designed and executed by Helen Rhoades. Photographed by John Norman.

Figure 5-6. "Virgin and Child." This terra cotta piece measures 1 foot high. Designed and executed by Jane McClintock. Photographed by Walter Russell.

Figure 5-4. "Brotherhood." A modern day ceramic mosaic depicting three figures with outstretched arms. Designed and executed by Wilcke Smith. Courtesy of the Newman Center, Albuquerque, New Mexico.

THE PRODUCTION POTTER

For the limited production potter who turns out perhaps six of a kind the opportunities are many.

Flower vases: All churches and synagogues use flowers during the year. The flowers require suitable containers for proper display and so do the florists who provide these flowers for sale. Pots in liturgical colors with suitable religious symbols would have a ready market. Special pots for baptismal flowers with the new baby's name and baptism date could become family heirlooms. Cemetery plant containers will last for several years and are more attractive than the usual run of the mill item provided by the florist or cemetery. Wedding vases, perhaps inscribed with the couple's names and their date of marriage, are simply not available except from craftsmen.

Lighting: If some of the best restaurants in America can commission production potters to provide original lighting fixtures, why, oh why, don't the churches and synagogues follow suit? All kinds of ceramic fixtures incorporating religious motifs and designs can be produced by production potters at costs that can easily compete with any commercial company producing fixtures in wood, metal, or enamel. Furthermore, the exact color desired can be had. There are also the Jewish Festival of Lights (Chanukah) and Christmas to consider. Special candleholders are needed for both holidays and for both indoor and outdoor use. Too many of the religious–oriented shops within the churches or synagogues feature only the commercial catalog items, many imported, when they could just as well be featuring the work of their local artisans.

Figure 5-7. This stylized menorah is made of unglazed red clay. The piece measures 13 inches in height and 22 inches wide at the top. Designed and executed by Riva H. Freed. Courtesy of Mr. and Mrs. Edmund Rubin.

Figure 5-8. Slip-washed in black clay, this menorah won an award at an exhibition at the Interchurch Center in New York City. The piece measures 1¼ feet tall and 1¼ feet wide at the top. Designed and executed by Riva H. Freed.

Figure 5-9. "Family." A wood and ceramic tile wall mural, measuring 6 by 7 feet. Exotic woods were combined with ceramic tiles to depict the enduring qualities of the family unit. At the left Jacob's family of twelve sons are shown. At the right is the tree of Jesse. Also represented are "homes in which thy people dwell," taken from a blessing, the representation (center) of the family — from birth to old age — and the symbol for infinity. Designed and executed by the Bartels. Courtesy of the University of Tennessee at Martin. Photographed by Vernon Matlock.

THE NONPRODUCTION POTTER

For those who create slab and sculptural forms—one of a kind items—there are equally as many exciting opportunities.

Seasonal items: Original Nativity sets will always have a ready market. So will menorahs, Chanukah lights, Seder cups and plates, and Christmas candleholders.

Liturgical vessels: A truly original work might be a baptismal font sculptured with figures or suitable flora and fauna. There are the lavabo (the ceremonial washing bowls used by the priest to wash his hands before Communion), ceramic alms boxes to hang on the wall, stations of the cross, a removable baptismal bowl to be used in the font, incense containers, bobeches (for protecting the tables from candle drippings), processional crosses, icons, stat-

ues, the piscina (the basin and drain for disposing of ablutions and for cleansing the chalice and paten), a pyx (the case used to carry the consecrated bread and wine of Communion to the sick), and sanctuary lamps.

Ceramic work also lends itself to mixed media for mural and wall decoration, as well as tiles and floor areas. It can be combined with wood, metal, and plastic in many mosaic arrangements and can be used in conjuction with lighted panels when it is combined with glass or plastic inserts. It has a natural affinity to stones and pebbles in floor pattern designs. It can even be used to create rosary beads and outdoor sculpture.

The work illustrated in this chapter represents only a small portion of the design ideas that are possible.

Figure 5-10. "Te Deum." This mural, measuring 12 feet wide, is actually carved brick with enamel inserts. Designed and executed by William Severson for Concordia Senior College, Fort Wayne, Indiana. Photographed by the artist.

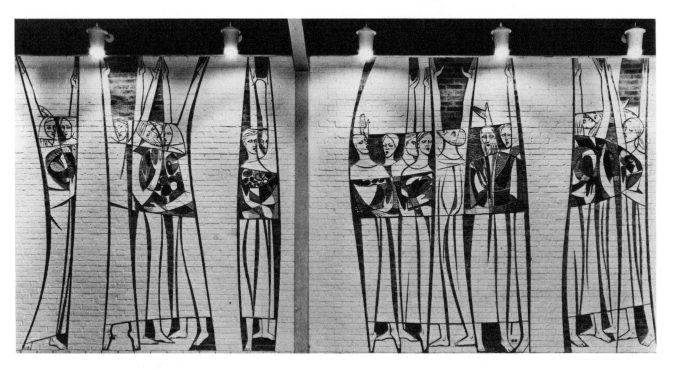

Figure 5-11. "Martyrs and Fighters." A memorial to those who died in the Nazi holocaust, this mosaic mural measures 10 by 23 feet. Written details of the mural are beneath the burning bush, which is surrounded by the supplicating hands. The left hand represents the feminine side of the family, which carries on the traditions of the home, while the right hand represents the male side of the family, creators of the law, music, and writing. The mosaic is composed of stoneware, glass, glazed clay, and natural stones. Each figure represented is a recognized martyr or hero from among the six million who died during the war. Each of the brass torches in the center represent one million deaths and each torch is lighted permanently. The work required two months of research for the artist. Designed and executed by Charles Clement for the Jewish Community Center, Tucson, Arizona.

63

CHAPTER 6.

ENAMEL AND METAL IN ECCLESIASTICAL CRAFTS

For centuries very rich, precious, and durable materials have enhanced houses of worship. Even prior to the Christian era gold and bronze were used by the Egyptians, Greeks, Romans, and Phoenicians to create idols, images, and containers used in worship practices. A great many of these antique enamels and metals have come down to us from past eras, preserving the techniques and designs used by other artists. It is interesting that many religious pieces, dating back from the sixteenth century to present times, are still used for their original purposes. St. Peter's in Rome holds only some of the outstanding examples with its magnificent bronze doors, gold chalices, and other works of art. We should also be reminded that Westminster Abbey in England, begun after the Battle of Hastings in 1066 A.D., has never really been completed to this day. It contains a history of several centuries' worth of art in metal and enamel created for religious purposes. In the past the churches and synagogues were patrons of the arts, as well as preservation museums in their own right. The craft guild system in Europe, from the Middle Ages through the seven-

teenth century, developed and preserved high standards of technique and design, which we in this century are only beginning to revive.

All kinds of metals have been used for religious art—gold, silver, and bronze being the most precious and most frequently used. Copper, brass, steel, aluminum, and other alloys have become more popular in this century, because new techniques for working with these metals have encouraged their use. Even the art of the ferrier or blacksmith has been revived for ornamental doors, gates, rails, and windows. Metal is worked in a number of processes, including forging, pouring, casting, welding, brazing, and soldering. It can be worked cold or heated and can be melted to liquid states for casting, so that under the control of the artist, it can be made to take any form desired and hold that form, design, and pattern for centuries.

Enamel is a form of glass, ground to fine granules, that can be fused to metal and clay under very high heat. Color is added to the grains to produce a wide range of hues and values. The process usually takes place in a kiln or high-heat oven. Chinese and Jap-

Figure 6-1. "Dona Nobis Pacem." This bronze figure can be thought of as either male or female, suggesting humanity in the general sense. The figure measures 1½ feet in height. Designed and executed by Perry Thomas. Photographed by the artist.

Figure 6-2. These altar lights, measuring 14 inches in height, are made of wrought and forged steel. Designed and executed by Jack Hemenway for All Saint's Church, South Burlington, Vermont. Photographed by Harriet R. Hemenway.

anese enamel techniques, showing a high level of expertise, have been known about for centuries. The glaze, placed upon ceramics in the kiln, is essentially the enameling process, since it is fused to the clay under heat. When the enameling process is used on metal, colors of great vibrancy are attained. Enameling techniques have been combined with metals such as gold, silver, and bronze for centuries.

Figure 6-4. "The Descent from the Cross." Station thirteen in a series of fourteen stations of the cross done in copper repoussé. Designed and executed by Charles Clement for St. Francis de Sales Catholic Church, Tucson, Arizona.

Figure 6-3. "Le Pere." This sterling silver and gold-washed chalice measures 11½ by 4½ inches. It is set with amethysts, and on the base appear the French words, "Le Pere," standing for Father, Son, and Holy Ghost. The first verse of the Book of John is written in French on the bowl portion. Designed and executed by Gerald R. Benedict. Cloth handwoven by Linda Benedict. Photographed by the artist.

Figure 6-5. This brass and enamel tester features a Eucharistic theme with stylized grapes, wheat, fish, and loaves, and the words "light" and "life." The tester design is continued onto the wall in latex and gold leaf. Designed and executed by Sister M. Hiltrudis, C.P.P.S. Photographed by the artist.

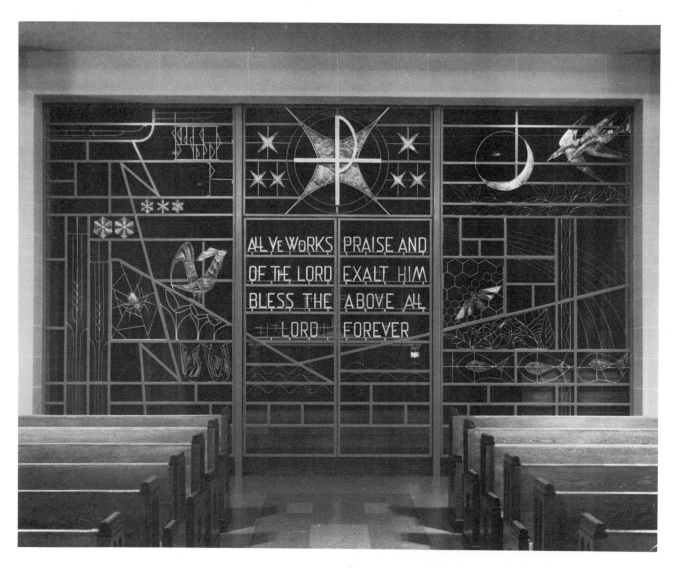

The grill reads:

ALL YE WORKS PRAISE AND
OF THE LORD EXALT HIM
BLESS THE ABOVE ALL
LORD FOREVER

Figure 6-6. This grill is made of brass, bronze, and silver with designed channeling. Designed and executed by Sister M. Hiltrudis, C.P.P.S. Courtesy of St. Mary's Institute, O'Fallon, Missouri. Photographed by the artist.

Figure 6-7. The shield, or breastplate, for the Torah is now a purely decorative item, though at one time it was used to indicate that a particular portion of the scroll had been rolled and readied for a specific holiday. The sole design of this 9-inch brass shield is the piercing with Hebrew letters in the negative spaces. The Hebrew reads, "The world rests on three foundations — justice, truth, and peace." The round shape was used to represent the universal element encompassing all peoples. Designed and executed by Renate F. Chernoff. Photographed by David E. Richer.

Figure 6-8. "In Honor of our Fathers." This bronze and marble menorah was created for the Chanukah festival. Measuring 27 by 20 inches, it uses the traditional olive oil for burning. It was the 1973 winner of the Beaux Arts Liturgical Award. Designed and executed by S.F. Canneto. Photographed by Mark Landsman.

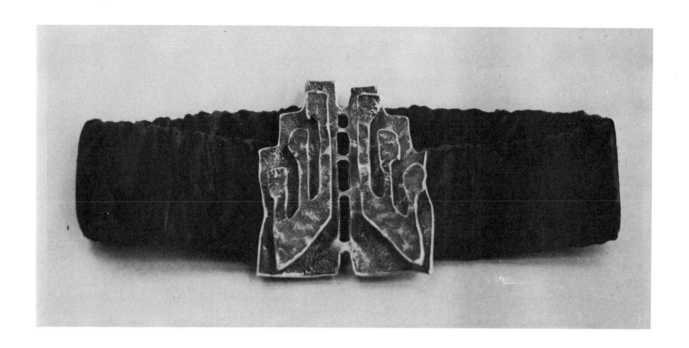

Figure 6-9. A Torah binder may be either a wimple-style, a long strip of cloth, or a simple strap with an attached clasp. It functions as a device to keep the scroll securely fastened. This sterling silver, reticulated buckle is an abstract rendering of the two tablets of the law, with the letter Shin and its mirror image standing for "the Almighty." The six flame-like projections of the letters represent the six million Jews killed in World War II. The Torah binder measures 4 by 3½ inches. Designed and executed by Renate F. Chernoff. Photographed by David E. Richer.

Figure 6-10. This Chanukah menorah was fabricated in welded mild steel. The projecting starter candle is used to light the other candles. The piece measures 2 by 1½ by 1½ feet. Designed and executed by Jack Hemenway. Photographed by Harriet R. Hemenway.

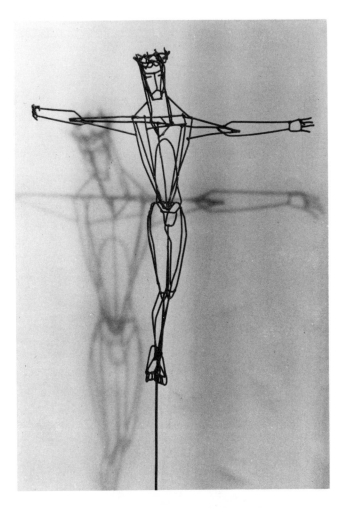

Figure 6-11. "Corpus." A 5½-foot welded steel crucifix, which has the engaging ability to create a line design in shadow on the surface behind it. Designed and executed by Perry Thomas. Photographed by the artist.

Figure 6-12. "Iron Cross." This cross was wrought in mild steel and welded. The entire piece measures 4 by 2½ feet. Designed and executed by Jack Hemenway for St. Dunstan's Church, Ellsworth, Maine. Photographed by Harriet R. Hemenway.

Figure 6-13. A hand-wrought sterling silver cross and chain with 14 karat gold over the end pieces, featuring moonstone in the center, as well as amethyst, tourmalines, and garnets. The size of the cross is 4 3/4 by 1 3/4 inches. Designed and executed by Vada Clark Beetler.

Figure 6-14. The cross is made of Blenko glass and metal.
It stands 22 by 13¼ inches. Designed by Mary Lloyd Black.
Photographed by Chet Hawes.

TERMINOLOGY

The United States of America is a country of specialists. By briefly defining the following terms for those who may not understand them, we hope to encourage an age of enlightenment for metal work in religious art.

Direct enamel: This is the process where color and glass grains are fused under high heat directly to a metal, such as silver, gold, brass, or copper. The process produces an enameled surface upon the metal, which can exhibit great color variety while maintaining the durability of the metal.

Cloisonné: This is the process of applying enamel between thin strips of metal (usually gold or silver) fixed to the edge. Silver and gold cloisonne wire are especially made for this purpose. They are formed into the design, placed upon the metal, and filled in with different-colored enamels. Finally, the piece is fired.

Champlevé: In champlevé enamel the design is carved directly into the metal and the depressions are filled in with enamel. The raised areas of metal which remain form the outlines of the design.

Plique-à-jour: Another process used in enamel techniques melts the enamel between areas of metal (holes) which are not backed by metal, so that after the enamel has been fired, a transparent area of the design appears as part of the total surface. Since there are both opaque and transparent enamels, it is possible to use both effects. In items such as cups and bowls both sides of the metal will show an enameled design when plique-à-jour methods are used.

Figure 6-16. A copper enamel plate done in amber, red, and white, using opaque and transparent colors. This 8-inch plate could be used as a Seder plate. Designed and executed by Barbara Hackett. Photographed by Ruth Carey.

Figure 6-15. A copper enamel cross done in swirling techniques. The background is black and the swirls are multicolored. Designed and executed by Barbara Hackett. Photographed by Ruth Carey.

74

Figure 6-17. This mezuzah was executed in welded and etched brass that had been blackened with a copper enamel insert. Designed and executed by Shirley and Howard Rosenthal for the Jewish Center of Greater Buffalo, Buffalo, New York.

Figure 6-18. "Reliquary." The 3- by 4½-inch cloisonné enamel box could be used as a wafer or bread container. Designed and executed by Margaret Fischer. Photographed by the artist.

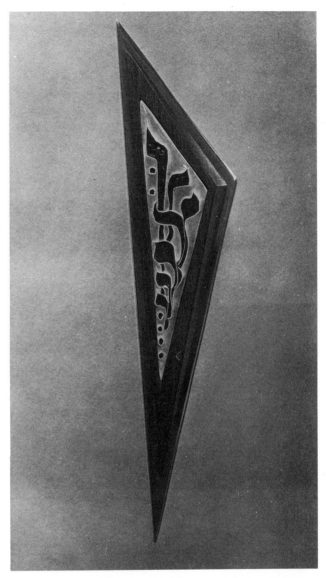

Figure 6-19. A cloisonné mezuzah on fine silver, mounted in walnut on sterling silver wire. The enamel colors are wine, scarlet, and ivory pink with foil inlays. The size is approximately 6 by 1¼ inches. Designed by Renate F. Chernoff. Courtesy of Mr. and Mrs. Mitchel Robinson. Photographed by David E. Richer.

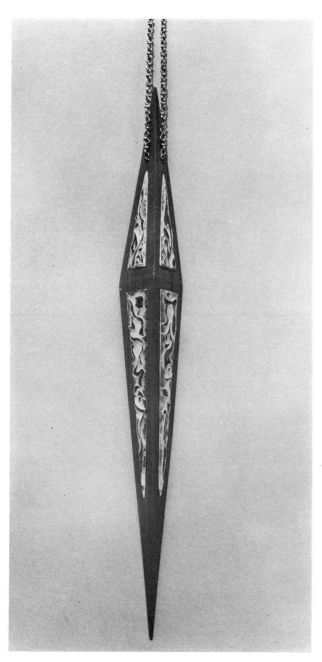

Figure 6-20. A contemporary Torah pointer using Hebrew calligraphy for the cloisonné inserts between walnuts. The Hebrew corresponds to the words justice, truth, peace, and love. Fine silver wire was used on fine silver metal. Designed and executed by Renate F. Chernoff. Photographed by David E. Richer.

Figure 6-21. A cast sterling silver mezuzah, measuring 3½ by ¾ inches. Designed by Renate F. Chernoff. Photographed by David E. Richer.

Casting: The act or process of pouring metal into a mold, cast, or dye in order to produce a prearranged shape or form is called casting. Lost-wax casting involves the preparation of a wax sculpture or form, which is melted out and refilled with the metal during the casting process. Exceedingly detailed work is produced in this way.

Forging: Forging is the process by which metal is heated to an intense heat and then hammered into a shape or form. Metal can also be cold-forged by hammering, but by heating the metal to cherry red color, such metals as iron are more easily shaped.

Figure 6-22. "Waiting for Elijah." A 8½-inch cast silver and bronze cup with fittings of coral, Osage orange, and ivory. It is used at Passover as a wine goblet and is set at an empty spot on the table as is customary for the arrival of the prophet Elijah. This is a tradition symbolizing hospitality. Designed and executed by S.F. Canneto. Photographed by Mark Landsman.

Figure 6-23. This Celtic cross is 3¾ inches with a 30-inch chain. It is gold-forged and constructed with rivets and movable circles that were created to represent continuity enfolded by the church (cross). The twelve rivets represent twelve apostles. Designed and executed by Carrie Adell for the Most Reverend William Jones, Bishop of St. Louis, Episcopal Diocese of Missouri. Photographed by Murray Warren.

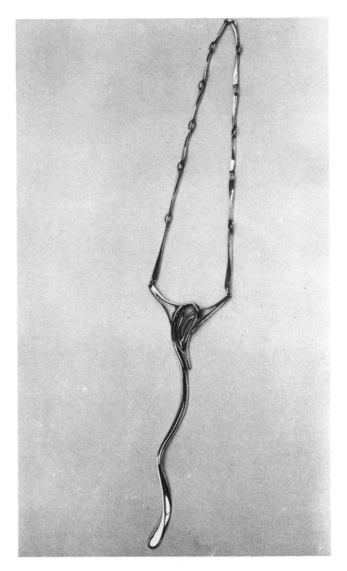

Figure 6-25. The inspiration for this Torah shield came from the Tree of Life motif (the Torah itself being referred to as a "tree of life to those who cling to its commandments") and the breastplate of the high priest Aaron with its twelve stones. Since the Torah is the basis of all ethical, moral, and just concepts — the root of all learning — an organic design reminiscent of a root system evolved. Tumbled stones, rather than cut stones, were used in clawlike, rather than regular and traditional, settings to carry out the theme. The shield, which is used on the front of the Torah, hanging over the mantel from the tops of the roller bars, measures 9 by 7¼ inches. Designed and executed by Renate F. Chernoff. Photographed by David E. Richer.

Figure 6-26. This 9- by 20-inch Torah pointer features a forged chain and a three-dimensional design in forged sterling silver with a smooth, flat back. The twelve sections of the chain were chosen to represent the twelve tribes of Israel. The letter Shin represents "the Almighty." Designed and executed by Renate F. Chernoff. Photographed by David E. Richer.

Figure 6-24. The main structure of this door is aluminum with a copper background that has attained a green patina. The door features stylized grapes and leaves and symbols for the beginning and the end. The verse "I am the vine, you are the branches," was the inspiration for the theme. A Chi Rho appears in the center area. Designed by Sister M. Hiltrudis, C.P.P.S. Courtesy of St. Mary's Institute, O'Fallon, Missouri. Photographed by the artist.

Figure 6-27. A sterling silver forged and fabricated chalice. Designed and executed by Sara Jayne Cole.

Soldering: Any metal or alloy that is melted and used for joining or binding metal surfaces together has been soldered.

Brazing: This is actually a soldering process, using a metal such as brass that has a very high melting point.

Fabricating: When a number of different metal processes are used in any one piece, it is said to have been fabricated.

There are tremendous uses for enamel and metal techniques in religious art. Museums, churches, and synagogues are filled with past examples, so it seems superfluous to offer suggestions for use. Metal combines well with many other materials besides enamel, such as wood, stone, glass, jewels, and fiber. We hope the illustrations in this chapter have provided many ideas.

Figure 6-28a and b. This chalice is constructed of gold-plated copper, silver, and brass on walnut and jade. It was executed in repoussé, raising, and etching, and was fabricated so that the container and chalice forms may be separated. The chalice has sections of pierced brass against purple plexiglass. Figure 6-28b shows the two sections separated. The piece is 8 inches in diameter and 10 inches tall. Designed and executed by Don M. Johnson. Photographed by the artist.

CHAPTER 7.

FIBER IN ECCLESIASTICAL CRAFTS

The term "fiber" encompasses a wide range of methods and materials from weaving, embroidery, and appliqué to lace making, macrame, and printing techniques. The great charm and vitality of fiber crafts comes from the vibrant use of color and great diversity of texture possible with them.

A large majority of the craft work produced for liturgical use in the past ten or fifteen years has been in fiber. Fiber art in religious application far exceeds clay, metal, or wood art simply because of the desire of so many churches and synagogues to bring in color. Since some of the fiber arts, such as appliqué and embroidery, provide means of adding color and design without the high cost of precious metals, for example, these areas have become increasingly popular. Appointments can be changed frequently, allowing for great diversity of design within the houses of worship.

Methods such as tapestry weaving, lace making, and metal-thread embroidery will always be far more costly than other fiber techniques due to the amount of time and expense of materials needed to create the work. Tapestry weaving on a large scale

for hangings and other appointments requires great amounts of time and patience. Embroidery, appliqué, and other combined techniques, however, which are used for many paraments, vestments, and articles used in services, take less time as a rule. Often the work can be designed by one artist and then divided up among the congregation and members.

Of all the embroidery methods, perhaps the canvas work medium, or needlepoint as it is so often called, requires the greatest amount of time. Yet, needlepoint has the longest wearing potential, and vast amounts of needlepoint, or canvas work, grace many churches and synagogues both here in America and in Europe. Macrame, though seen in many churches and synagogues abroad, has not seen the great interest here in America that other fiber methods have. Since it can be made from manmade fibers with tremendous strength and wearing potentials, more consideration should be given to macrame as a creative fiber form.

Special liturgical appointments, such as equipment for weddings, funerals, and baptisms, offer a

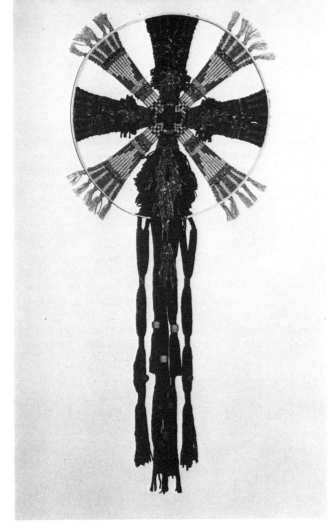

Figure 7-1. "Chrismon." The designer of this tapestry, which was woven over a split white oak hoop, felt that off-loom weaving would be a new and interesting way to interpret Christian symbols. The wall decoration consists of the Greek X, or Chi, standing for Jesus, and a cross enclosed in the circle. It was done in rust, dark browns, and earth tones of wool and acrylic yarns and is enhanced by the unglazed clay beads on the tassels. The piece is 21 inches in diameter. Designed and executed by Anne Sharpe. Courtesy of Mr. and Mrs. John K. Munro. Photographed by Terry C. Domm.

Figure 7-2. The Trinity tapestry was designed to hang in front of a recessed tabernacle. The tapestry hangs on a pulley system, so that it can be raised and lowered to expose or cover the tabernacle area. Woven in blacks, browns, grays, and whites, it serves as a symbol of mysterious presence. The warp, which is four-ply jute, is exposed in sections, and the piece was worked in panels to allow for partial revelation and partial concealment of the tabernacle area behind. The descending triangle motif symbolizes the Trinity in the Eucharist. The weft of the tapestry is wool, and copper wire was used for accent. The overall size is 7 by 9 feet. Designed and executed by Douglas E. Fuchs.

wide range of design ideas. The possibilities are endless. Hangings, banners, and wall decorations of all styles and designs can serve a multitude of functions. Any number of techniques or methods may be used in their creation, and they need not be flat. Often banners are enhanced by a three-dimensional scheme.

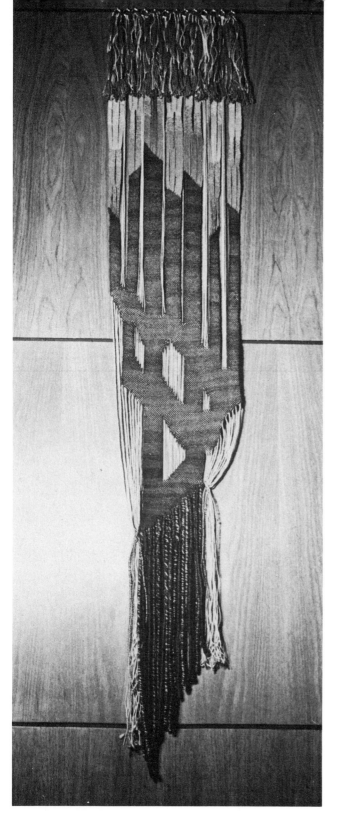

Figure 7-3. "Hanging Menorah I." The menorah has undergone a transformation from a purely functional item to a symbolic one. Usually, it is represented in metal, clay, or wood, but here it has been woven in wools and unspun fleece, using some copper and brass wire in wrapped areas. The menorah is 1 1/3 by 6 2/3 feet, and the colors are shades of brown, black, orange, yellow, and natural linen. Designed and executed by Renate F. Chernoff. Collection of Mr. and Mrs. Bernard Bernstein. Photographed by David E. Richer.

Figure 7-4. This pulpit hanging was designed for use during Lent and Advent. It is 3 2/3 by 1 1/2 feet and is woven in linen, wool, and rayon with dukagang inlay. The hanging represents the receptive soul, as in the ancient attitude of prayer with arms outstretched upward. Designed and executed by Marjorie Pohlman. Courtesy of Berea Lutheran Church, Richfield, Minnesota. Photographed by Charles Pohlman.

Figure 7-5. This pulpit hanging was intended for Sundays after Pentecost. It is woven of wool, linen, and rayon with dukagang inlay. The design depicts leaf and growth, so it is used during the Trinity season when emphasis is placed on growing in the way of the Lord. It also represents the parable of the wine and the branches. The piece measures 1 1/2 by 3 2/3 feet. Designed and executed by Marjorie Pohlman. Courtesy of Berea Lutheran Church, Richfield, Minnesota. Photographed by Charles Pohlman.

Figure 7-6. This pulpit hanging, measuring 13 by 56 inches, was woven in textured rayon threads. It hangs directly over the pulpit in view of the congregation and utilizes the colors mentioned in the Bible for the tabernacle in the wilderness. The design is organic in nature and universal in concept. Designed by Renate F. Chernoff. Photographed by David E. Richer.

Figure 7-7. This altar super-frontal was designed for the Pentecost. It hangs in front of the altar, but never reaches the floor, and is especially suited to altars that have other carving or decoration that should be exposed. It is handwoven, in linen, rayon, and wool, and measures 1 by 10 feet. Designed and executed by Marjorie Pohlman. Courtesy of Berea Lutheran Church, Richfield, Minnesota. Photographed by Charles Pohlman.

Figure 7-8. A tapestry woven tallis in man-made fibers. The Hebrew inscription at the neck band is the priestly blessing used in both Judaism and Christianity and reads, "May the Lord bless you and keep you. May the Lord make his countenance to shine upon you and be gracious unto you. May the Lord lift up his countenance upon you and give you peace." The prayer shawl measures 1 2/3 by 7 2/3 feet and was done in off-white, purple, and silver. The fringes at the four corners of the shawl must be wrapped and tied in accordance with biblical law, and the mixing of wool and linen is frowned upon by Orthodox and Conservative congregations. Designed and executed by Renate F. Chernoff. Photographed by David E. Richer.

Figure 7-9. The embroidery stitches on this woolen, off-white tallis were done on canvas at the neck edge and the four corners. The tent stitch was used for all the ornamentation and the lettering. The motifs represent the seven indigenous fruits of Israel — wheat, barley, pomegranates, dates, figs, olives, and grapes. The lettering is a shortened version taken from Psalms 137:5 "If I forsake thee oh Jerusalem, may my right hand forsake its cunning." The tallis measures 3 by 4 feet. Designed and executed by Tova Messing. Photographed by Mort Tucker.

Figure 7-10. A needlepoint bag, 9½ by 10½ inches, in which to carry the tallis, worked in green and red in silk, crewel yarns, and metallic threads. The stitches used were the tent, flat, and backstitches on #24 mono canvas. The Star of David in the design contains the Hebrew word for life. On the reverse side of the tallis bag the Hebrew lettering reads, "Brian Keith, son of Marvin Lee, April 27, 1974." The bag was presented by the artist to her son on the occasion of his Bar Mitzvah. Designed and executed by Carol Frumhoff. Photographed by Tom Stewart.

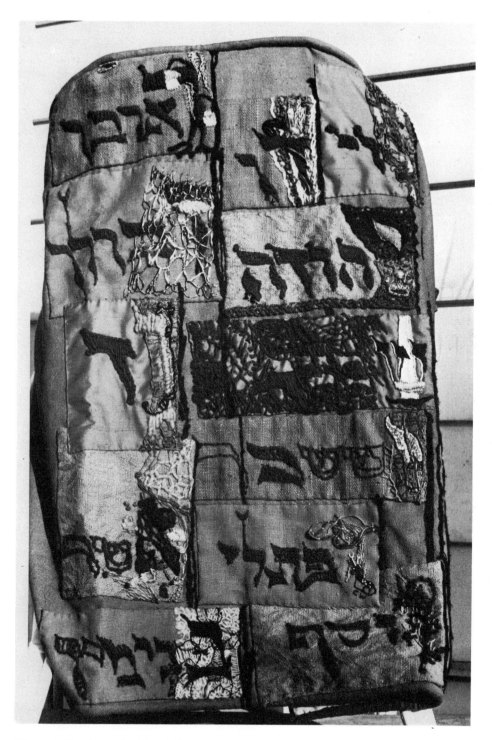

Figure 7-11. An embroidered Torah mantel executed in mixed threads on a linen background fabric. Designed and executed by Joan Koslan Schwartz and her students. Photographed by Ben Schwartz.

Figure 7-13. This canvas work curtain, done in two sections, was stitched in DMC wools with beads added. The Hebrew lettering reads, "Hallelujah." The curtain measures 4 3/4 by 4 1/3 feet. Designed by Amiram Shanir. Executed by Ita Aber. Courtesy S.A.R. Academy, Riverdale, New York.

Figure 7-14. A white wool parament, measuring 2 1/3 by 2 2/3 feet. This hanging for a pulpit is one of a set of four pairs (see the other part of this pair in Figure 7-15). The hanging is richly embroidered with a phoenix and many crosses. Its mate, the butterfly, hangs to the right of it when in use. Both are done in hot pinks, oranges, lemons, and violet. Designed and executed by Wilcke Smith. Photographed by the artist. Courtesy of St. Paul's Lutheran Church, Albuquerque, New Mexico.

Figure 7-12. This Torah binder was embroidered on linen fabric. Designed by Bucky King. Executed by Lillian Freehof for the Rodelf Shalom Temple, Pittsburgh, Pennsylvania. Photographed by W.S. King.

Figure 7-16. The chalice veil cover uses appliqué and metal-thread embroidery techniques on a silk and linen background. The stylized cross motif is white, the appliqué cross is in shades of red and gold. The cover measures 20 inches square. Designed and executed by Bucky King. Photographed by W.S. King.

Figure 7-15. The accompanying piece to the parament shown in Figure 7-14. This richly embroidered butterfly and cross are on a white wool background fabric. Designed and executed by Wilcke Smith. Photographed by the artist.

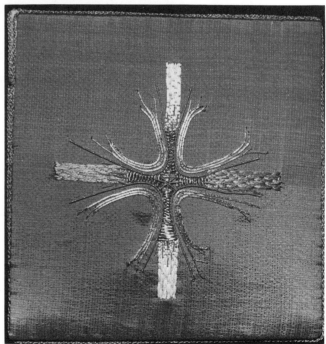

Figure 7-17. A 9-inch square burse to match the chalice veil set in Figure 7-16. The burse is red with silk and metal-thread embroidery in a cross form. Designed and executed by Bucky King. Photographed by W.S. King.

Figure 7-18a and b. A very handsome altar frontal of hand-dyed, braided nylon cord. It depicts the butterfly for eternal life and resurrection within Christianity. Detail is shown in Figure 7-18b. Designed and executed by Joan Michaels-Paque for St. Charles Borromeo Catholic Church, Milwaukee, Wisconsin. Photographed by the artist.

Figure 7-19. "The Multitude." An abstract macrame wall hanging worked in white cotton cord. Represented from the bottom up are a cross, two fish, five loaves of bread, and the multitudes. The piece measures 32 by 83 inches. Designed and executed by Bea Ingwersen. Photographed by Craig L. Meyer.

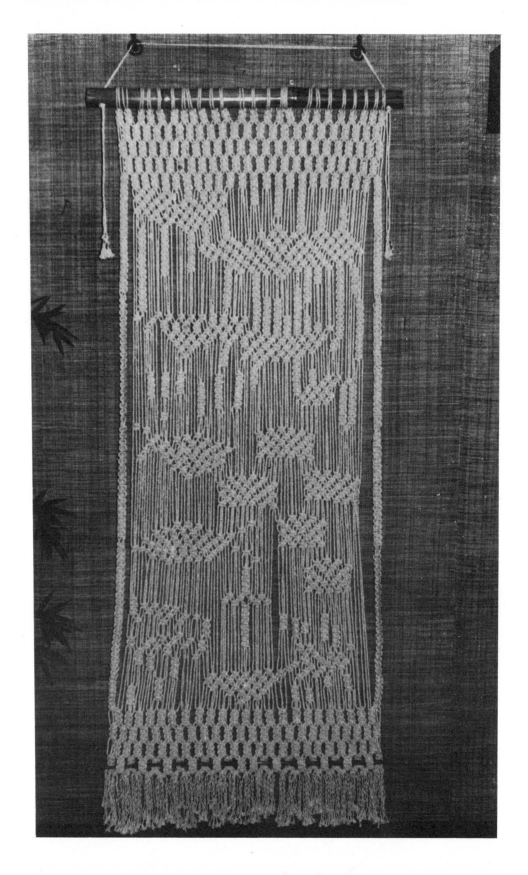

Captions for Color Plates

Plate 1. "Angel." An appliqué collage measuring 13 by 17 inches. Designed and executed by Margaret Cusack.

Plate 2. An appliqué wall hanging on black velvet, with large Hebrew letters spelling out the names Abraham, Isaac, and Jacob. Wishing to convey the continuity of Jewish belief, beginning with the patriarchs and continuing through the twelve tribes of Israel, the artist chose the following wording for the smaller lettering, "The Lord shall reign forever your God, o Zion, for all generations." Designed and executed by Bebe Brown for Temple Brith Shalom, Springfield, Illinois. Photographed by the artist.

Plate 3. "Brown Moon." A stitchery hanging depicting the creation, suitable for a chapel hanging or behind a baptismal font. Designed and executed by Phyllis I. Danielson. Photographed by the artist.

Plate 4. This Celtic cross is 3 ¾ by 4 inches with a 30-inch chain. It is gold-forged and constructed with rivets and movable circles that represent the twelve apostles. Designed and executed by Carrie Adell for the Most Reverend William Jones, Bishop of St. Louis, Episcopal Diocese of Missouri.

Plate 5. This menorah is 5 1/3 feet long and executed in bronze. Designed and executed by Arlene Abend. Courtesy of Temple B'nai Israel. Photographed by the artist.

Plate 6. One of a set of paraments designed to be used for the seasons of the church year. They were done in a trapezoid shape to better conform to the triangular altar and were worked in wool in a variety of embroidery techniques. The design on this one is the descending dove, standing for the Holy Ghost. Designed and executed by Wilcke Smith. Courtesy of St. Paul's Lutheran Church, Albuquerque, New Mexico.

Plate 7. "Continuation." A large stitchery and appliqué hanging depicting the Tree of Life and a sense of growing. It measures 3½ by 6½ feet. Designed and executed by Phyllis I. Danielson.

Plate 8. A sterling silver locket with moonstones, ivory, labradorite, and pearls. It was Masonite die-formed and chased. The double-hinged locket opens on both sides. The height of the locket is 3 inches; the width is 2½ inches. Designed and executed by G.P. van Duinwyk.

Plate 9. A sterling silver locket done in plique-à-jour enamel technique. It features ivory and moonstone and was Masonite die-formed and chased. The locket cover in front and rear are removable. The design symbolizes a man with outstretched arms, upside down. The enamel indicates the spirit of man and God. Plique-à-jour enamels are transparent, thus allowing light to be reflected through from the rear locket cap. The latter is the enamel in the concave and focuses light through the rear of the enamel in the direction of the viewer. Designed and executed by G.P. van Duinwyk. This piece was purchased by the Oakland Museum, Oakland, California.

Plate 10. This frontal measures 11 1/3 feet by 3 1/8 feet. It was done in hand appliqué, using fabric collage methods with silks, satins, velvets, gold kid, and wools. Designed and executed by Connie Eggers for the Washington Cathedral, Washington, D.C. Photographed by J. Alexander.

Plate 11. "Brotherhood." A ceramic mosaic in the shape of a cross with four hands joined in brotherhood. Designed and executed by Wilcke Smith. Collection of Mr. Robert Sanders.

Plate 12. A ceramic chalice and paten (Communion plate) together with a wine container and a water container. Designed and executed by Nancy and George Wettlaufer.

Plate 1

Plate 2

Plate 3

Plate 4

Plate 5

Plate 6

Plate 7

Plate 8

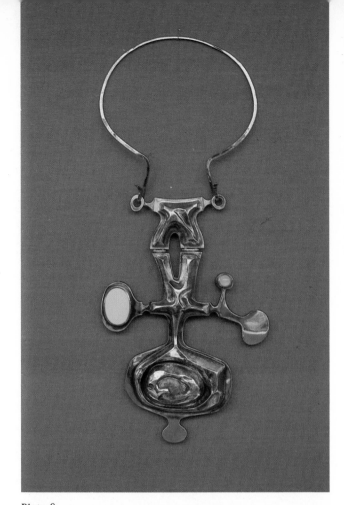

Plate 9

Plate 10

Plate 11

Plate 12

Plate 13

Plate 14

Plate 15

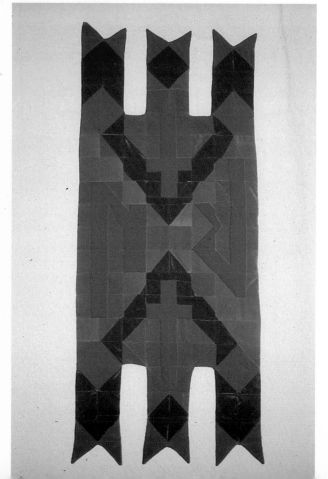

Plate 16

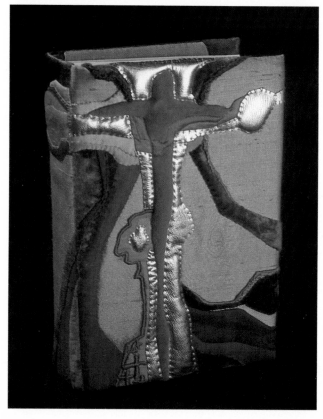

Plate 13. Another of a set of paraments (see Plate 6) done in a number of embroidery techniques. This one features the wheat and two crosses, standing for the Trinity season. Designed and executed by Wilcke Smith. Courtesy of St. Paul's Lutheran Church, Albuquerque, New Mexico.

Plate 14. A raised sterling silver chalice with 24 karat gold-plating on the inside of the cup, using the lost-wax casting method to cast the center section. Designed and executed by Walter Soellner. Courtesy of the North Carolina National Bank as part of its contemporary art collection.

Plate 15. A patchwork altar cloth, consisting of 281 fabric pieces in cotton, using close value hues. The side strips on the right and left hang down, when the cloth is in place on the altar. Designed and executed by Sidney Weeter for the Willow Grove United Methodist Church, Willow Grove, Pennsylvania.

Plate 16. A Bible cover, 9 by 6 by 3 inches, in appliqué and fabric collage. Designed and executed by Connie Eggers for the Washington Cathedral, Washington, D.C. The Bible cover was shown in the Guild for Religious Architecture Juried Show in 1975. Photographed by Allen Photos.

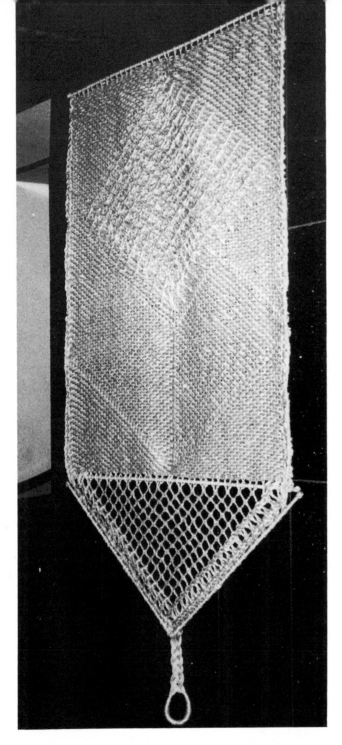

Figure 7-21. Our contemporary times often demand something more creative than a mere bridal veil. This bridal headdress, made of lutestring, old lace, and ribbons, features delightful quotations from the Bible stitched in silk thread in the Roumanian stitch on the various ribbons. On the back is the quote, "A man shall leave his mother and father, cleave to his wife and become one flesh." On one side the quotation reads, "Whither thou goest, I goest." A quote from "Godspell" says, "Finally glad that you are here by my side." Designed by Jorjanna Lundgren.

Figure 7-22. A gold silk and synthetic chasuble and stole with red and gold velvet shapes and couched gold and wool threads. The same design appears on the back. The chasuble is 46 inches long. Designed and executed by Margery Cosgrove for Christ's Church, Cincinnati, Ohio. Photographed by Robert Cosgrove.

Figure 7-20. "Interplay." A natural sissal hanging done in twining and bobbin lace techniques. It was created for space behind an altar and measures 6½ by 10½ feet. Designed by Evelyn B. Prosser.

Figure 7-24. A macrame stole in gold, using cottons, wool, and synthetic fibers. The stole measures 38 inches in length. Designed and executed by Margery Cosgrove for Christ's Church, Cincinnati, Ohio. Photographed by Robert Cosgrove.

Figure 7-23. Chasuble and stole. A red circular chasuble and stole in linen, cotton, rayon, and wool. The stole is circular in the old style — the forerunner of the modern stole — and was shaped on the loom. Both handwoven pieces may be worn together or separately. Designed and executed by Marna Lydecker for Christ Chapel, Gustavius Adolphus College, St. Peter, Minnesota.

Figure 7-25. This simple handwoven dalmatic was executed in cotton and wool. It emphasizes the role of the minister as a servant among the people. Designed and executed by Marna Lydecker for the Reverend Howard Amundson, St. Peter, Minnesota. Photographed by Wayne Schmidt.

Figure 7-26. A linen chasuble and stole with three fish embroidered in wool. It measures 46 inches long. Designed and executed by Margery Cosgrove for Christ's Church, Cincinnati, Ohio. Photographed by Robert Cosgrove.

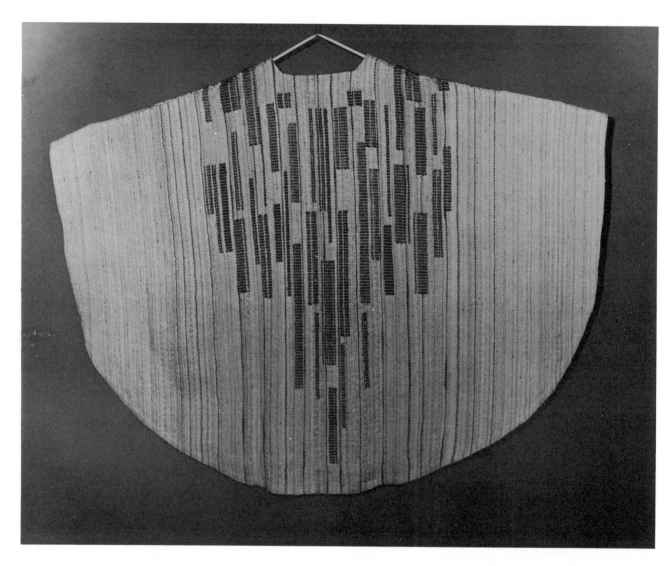

Figure 7-27. A chasuble woven in wool, linen, and cotton with dukagang inlay sections to raise the vertical stripes. It measures 3 by 5 feet. Designed and executed by Marjorie Pohlman. Courtesy of the Reverend Paul Lindstrom, Peace Lutheran Church, Wayland, Massachusetts. Photographed by Charles Pohlman.

106

Figure 7-28. "Parable of the Sower." A beautiful banner
done in silk screen on linen. It won the Best of Show Award
at the 1974 Religious Art Festival in Oak Ridge, Tennessee.
It measures 3 3/4 by 6 feet. Designed and executed by
Richard Daehnert. Photographed by the artist.

Figure 7-29. A batik angel banner on cotton, measuring 3 by 4½ feet. Designed and executed by Judy Elwood. Photographed by Ruth Carey.

Figure 7-30. "Lot's Wife." A double-weave banner with the pick up design in wool taken from a woodcut the artist did in graduate school. The piece won an award at the Columbus Liturgical Art Show V. It measures 27 by 79 inches. Designed by Judy Felgar. Photographed by Wayne Felgar.

Figure 7-31. An appliqué and embroidered Pentecostal banner with the words, "You will receive power," stitched at the bottom. Designed and executed by Deborah Anderson. Courtesy of the First Congregational Church, Columbus, Ohio.

Figure 7-32. A banner in appliqué, using the cross shape as the banner shape. Designed by Lorna Paul. Courtesy of St. Francis Catholic Church, Jefferson, North Carolina. Photographed by Philip Paul.

Figure 7-33. "You Can't Beat God for Imagination." A felt appliqué banner, 2 by 4 feet, using a snowflake motif, because no two snowflakes are ever identical. Designed and executed by Peggy Haaland Heddleson. Photographed by Ruth Carey.

Figure 7-34. "The Lord Delights in You." A felt and cloth
appliqué banner with flower motifs, because flowers are
one of the delights in nature for both sight and smell. It
measures 3 by 5 feet. Designed and executed by Peggy
Haaland Heddleson. Photographed by Ruth Carey.

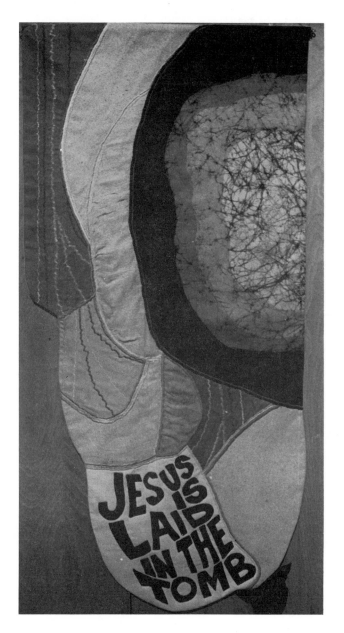

Figure 7-35a and b. "Jesus is Lain in the Tomb" and "Veronica Wipes the Face of Jesus." Two of a series of fourteen hangings for the stations of the cross, using batik details and gauze overlays on hand-appliquéd letters. They are done in shades of white and yellow and were made to complement their setting. Only abstract forms and lettering were used to convey the messages. Designed and executed by Jorjanna Lundgren.

Figure 7-36. This Nativity hanging features canvas work that was appliqued to white fabric with an embroidered star. It is used during the Advent season and measures 1½ by 4½ feet. Designed and executed by Bucky King. Photographed by W.S. King.

Figure 7-37. A Christmas banner in red, orange, and golds, using calligraphy done in appliqué. The letters spell out "Joy to the World, the Lord Has Come." Designed and executed by Marna Lydecker. Courtesy of Union Presbyterian Church, St. Peter, Minnesota. Photographed by Wayne Schmidt.

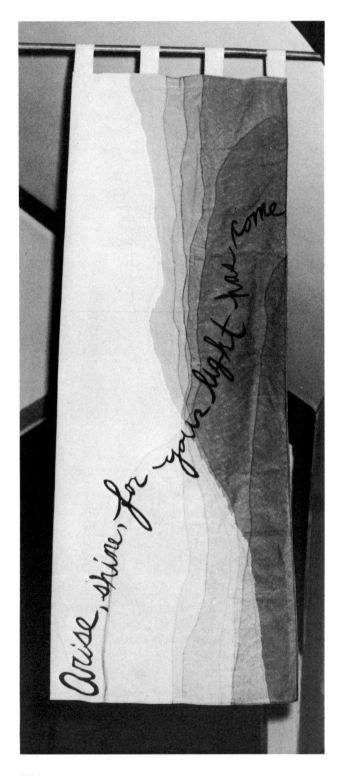

Figure 7-38. An Epiphany banner made in cotton, polyester knit, nylon net, and felt. The lettering refers to the Epiphany message and the spreading of the Gospel (or light) throughout the world. Designed and executed by Marna Lydecker for the Union Presbyterian Church, St. Peter, Minnesota.

Figure 7-39. "Fishers of Men." A handcrafted leather wall hanging, 1 by 2 1/3 feet, in goatskin, calfskin, and pigskin over plywood. The design is composed of an outline of the fish with three crosses representing Simon, Peter, and Andrew. The inspiration for the piece was the verse in Matthew 4:18-19. Designed and executed by Barbara W. Pullen. Photographed by Ruth Carey.

Figure 7-40. "What We Preach." An appliqué hanging done in many fabrics. The text was taken from 1 Cor. 4:5, "What we preach is not ourselves, but Jesus Christ as Lord with Ourselves as servants for Jesus' sake." The appliqué measures 3 by 7 feet. Designed and executed by Nell Battle Booker Sonneman. Photographed by Charlie Brown.

Figure 7-41. "Woman Clothed With Sun." A 6-foot tall, appliqué and multifabric hanging. The text was taken from Apoc. 12, "Woman clothed with sun and the moon under her feet and a crown of twelve stars upon her head." Designed and executed by Nell Battle Booker Sonneman. Photographed by Charlie Brown.

Figure 7-42a, b, c, and d. "Perchance to Dream." This fantastic angel is worked over metal tubing, wire, and styrofoam in a tremendous assortment of white and off-white threads, using appliqué, crochet, macrame, knotless netting, needleweaving, and buttonhole stitching techniques. It speaks strongly for the totally three-dimensional approach in fibers for liturgical material. The piece is 6½ by 9½ feet around. Designed and executed by Nancy and Dewey Lipe. Photographed by Dewey Lipe.

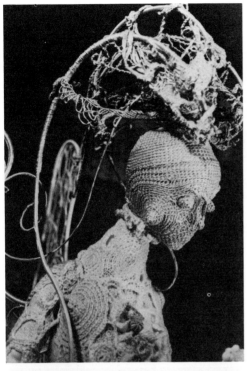

Figure 7-43. "Metamorphosis." A large sculptural piece in many materials, using machine-quilting, hand-stitching, appliqué, crochet, buttonhole wraps, needleweaving, and padding over a wire form. The butterfly is the symbol of eternity. The piece measures 7½ feet tall and 5 feet wide. Designed and executed by Nancy and Dewey Lipe. Photographed by Dewey Lipe.

CHAPTER 8.

WOOD IN ECCLESIASTICAL CRAFTS

Wood is very close to the world God created and has been symbolized in religion in the form of the Tree of Life. Wooden crosses have been used for centuries to represent the cross upon which Christ was crucified. It has been in years past the actual building material used in churches and synagogues and continues in this capacity today. The rich patterns and warm patina of wood are pleasing to both the eye and hand. During the Middle Ages countless numbers of wood statues were carved and used as religious decorations. Noah built his ark of wood. Hundreds of churches and synagogues use wood for their doors, as well as arks, altars, pulpits, and lecturns. Many of the great cathedrals in Europe have interiors that took many years of carving to produce. Both rare and humble native lumber has been used to provide us with a wealth of carvings, architectural interiors, and exteriors, as well as the printing medium for numerous woodcuts.

By its very nature, wood can be carved, sanded, glued, rubbed, nailed, stamped, inlaid, burned, and laminated. It yields easily to most cutting tools and, like ceramics, the raw product is not costly.

It takes its beauty, patina, and form from the hand of the artist who is working on it. The aging process enhances the luster and color of wood over long periods of time, and it is readily available in many forms. Since it combines beautifully with many other materials, such as metal, glass, enamel, ceramics, plastic, and acrylics, the potential uses are limitless. Mosaics using wood as the sole material have only recently been used in a contemporary way for religious purposes. Yet, this area of mosaic work in wood and mixed media is one in which far more experimentation should be done.

There are basically two kinds of woods—the softwoods, or those belonging to the conifae family, such as firs and pines, and the hardwoods, belonging to the dicotyledonae family, or broad-leafed varieties. Since wood contains water within its cells, it must be seasoned before use and is, therefore, air- or kiln-dried. After seasoning, it is converted into lumber by the manner in which it is cut. There are as many kinds of wood as we have trees and all produce different color varieties and patinas.

Each year hundreds of new churches or synagogues are built or remodeled; yet few wood-carvers

Figure 8-1a and b. "Christ Glorified." A freestanding mahogany crucifix with a negative (b) side and a positive (a) side. The cross is 22 by 22 inches. Designed and executed by Jane McClintock for Christ Church, Lexington, Kentucky. Photographed by Walter Russell.

or wood craftsmen are called in to enhance these buildings with wood art. It has, instead, become too easy to simply consult one of the commercial catalogs which offer pews, chairs, altars, pulpits, lecturns, and even coffins at mass-production prices. The catalog companies might be well advised to seek the services of some of our wood craftsmen in order to raise the standard of their products. Often the wood craftsman can compete on equal footing in the cost area with mass-produced work. Perhaps a few ideas for the use of wood in ecclesiastical situations is needed to start both clergyman and craftsman thinking.

Figure 8-2. "St. John and Angel (Apocalypse)." A 3-foot-high wood carving in sycamore. Designed and executed by Jane McClintock. Courtesy of E. Rosenstark. Photographed by Walter Russell.

Figure 8-3. "St. Andrew." A wood relief carving in 2-inch-thick Philippine mahogany. The piece measures 5 by 2½ feet. Designed and executed by Marion George for St. Andrew's Brotherhood, St. Matthew's Episcopal Church, Pampa, Texas.

PRODUCTION WOODWORKERS

Since a great many craftsmen turn out bowls, furniture, tools, and other handcrafted items, using machine tools as well as hand tools, they might also consider these areas of production.

Furniture: Acolyte kneeling benches, which usually come in pairs, processional crosses, missal stands, Bible stands, hymn boards, credence tables, chapel pews, bulletin boards, altar desk stands for holding prayer books, alms boxes, litany desks, lighting fixtures, pew racks for hymnals, and window moldings are just a few ideas.

Building materials: Stamped and turned lumber, lathe-designed pillars, and trims of all kinds for interior use are needed.

Figure 8-4. "St. Matthew." A 5- by 2½-foot wood relief carving of St. Matthew done in 3-inch-thick mahogany. Designed and executed by Marion George for St. Matthew's Episcopal Church, Pampa, Texas.

Figure 8-5. This wall-hung crucifix was carved and constructed in walnut. It measures 2½ by 2½ feet. Designed and executed by Jane McClintock. Photographed by Walter Russell.

NONPRODUCTION CARVERS

Most wood-carvers do not produce great numbers of originals simply because of the time and work involved. But there will always be a market for hand-carving in statues, sculpture, printing, and joining.

Sculpture: Bishop's staffs, crucifixes, lecturns, pulpits, altars, arks, ark doors, Torah pointers, menorahs, ambrys, baptismal fonts, litany desks, alms bowls, murals, Nativity sets, stations of the cross, vigil lights, and candleholders are possibilities.

Printing: Wood block printing could be very effectively used for ecclesiastical art in church and synagogue programs, leaflets, holiday cards, posters, and in religious education.

Mixed media: Some of the new laminating techniques can be used effectively in doors and arches, forming patterns in specific designs. Floor inlays with wood and stone or ceramic wear as well as wall-to-wall carpeting. Murals for exteriors or interiors can combine wood and metal or clay. Glass and wood offer beautiful contrasts. Hand-carved letters set on stone or metal are truly more lovely than plastic numbers on a bulletin board facing the lawn of the church or synagogue. Small religious hand-carved jewelry combined with silver mounts or semiprecious stones might sell well in religious shops.

Figure 8-6a and b. "Meditation I." A freestanding cross form with a negative (a) and a positive (b) side, so that the cross may be turned about. The piece was carved in mahogany and measures 1½ by 1½ feet. Designed and executed by Jane McClintock. Photographed by Walter Russell.

Figure 8-7. "Nativity." A print from a woodcut, which might easily be used as a Christmas gift idea for many churches. The commissioning of exclusive and limited edition prints by churches and synagogues has not had widespread acceptance, but does offer a unique opportunity for the congregation, general public, and artist. Designed and executed by Rita McCarthy.

Figure 8-8. "Betrayal, Supper, Death." A mixed media assemblage in plywood and assorted found objects, measuring 8 by 4 feet. Designed and executed by Douglas E. Fuchs for the La Salle School Chapel, Albany, N.Y. Photographed by Brother Charles Hoffman, F.S.C.

123

Perhaps one of the reasons craft and artwork is not used more for liturgical purposes is because the clergy and clergy-oriented committees do not know the craftsman is out there. Craft artists should band together in order to make their talents known. The already organized craft guilds in this country could do much to promote their members in the ecclesiastical fields by very simple and inexpensive advertising.

In seeking photographs to illustrate contemporary wood work, we discovered that this was the only area in which an abundance was lacking. Hopefully, the work we've shown here will inspire others.

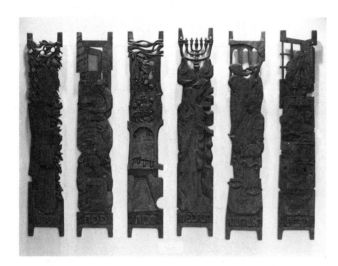

Figure 8-9a, b, c, and d. "Festival of Holidays." A set of six carved panels depicting the holidays of the Hebrew year. These panels, which are hung in the temple foyer leading to the educational wing, serve both as decorative and informative objects for the young people going to and from Hebrew school. Though done in birch, they are finished in walnut to comply with other wood in the surrounding area. Each panel is 63 inches high. Figure 8-9a shows the detail of the Passover panel; 8-9c is the Yom Kippur panel detail; 8-9d is the Succoth panel detail. Designed and executed by Jerry L. Caplan. Courtesy of Temple Emanuel, Pittsburgh, Pennsylvania.

CHAPTER 9.

WHEN, WHERE, WHAT, AND WHY

Art and religion have had a working companionship since early biblical times, as is evidenced by the specific instructions for the building of the first temple. Dr. Theodore Gill, Provost of John Jay College in New York City cites the verse from Solomon in the Old Testament (1 Kings 10:22). Solomon instructs the ships to bring back all manner of needed goods, including "apes, ivory, and peacocks." Solomon was noted for his wisdom; he obviously realized the necessity for such frivolities as monkeys for entertainment, ivory for enrichment and beautification, and peacocks for the sheer splendor of their magnificent tails. Though this is not actually stated in the biblical text, reading this portion of the Bible can only lead one to realize that all people need refreshment for their minds, bodies, and spirits, as well as their hearts and eyes.

The miracles in the New Testament give an indication of Christ's involvement with the arts. His garments, as he hung on the cross, were finely woven without seam. The guards cast lots for their ownership, which indicates the value and appeal of such garments. Christ turned water into wine at the Wedding Feast, and a ring was placed upon the finger of the Prodigal Son upon his return. All these things attest in written form to Christ's response to the unnecessary, the frivolous, and yet those very things that bring joy and beauty to life.

Religion has profited greatly by the contributions of past artists in architecture, painting, metal work, carving, ceramic work, fiber work, and glass work. Perhaps one of the major functions of art in religion has been in the keeping alive of the novelty and vividness of their relationship. Arts and crafts in religion are a testimonial to what we are all pulling for—the involvement of man and spirit. The directions and quality of our public and private lives are influenced by what we see and how we see it; religious craft work provides a way for the artist to express himself and a new way of seeing for the viewer.

All of us can be a part of the movement to make art and religion work together for our mutual benefit. By educating the clergy and integrating art into religious programs we'll be off to a good start. The use of contemporary graphic art for printed religious materials, the introduction of good contemporary art into Sunday school and religious education programs, the inclusion of religious art categories in all open juried exhibitions, the formation of state art liturgical councils and commissions, the inclusion of religious art on the agenda of all national and regional conferences, the preparation of catalog files for local art groups who have active religious artists, and, finally, the keeping alive of a vivid and new approach to all creativity will result in a renewed and revitalized partnership between religion and crafts.

Finally, we come to the "why" in "When, Where, What, and Why." The "why" is this: Because art helps men to relate to each other. The preoccupation with one's ego seen in the past decade might dwindle were we to use our interests in the arts to satisfy our individual souls. We are in need of a new sensitivity, which has been indicated by the back-to-nature movement. The activity generated by an art conscious society generates equal interest in life and all its multifaceted and varied creations. The arts are a memory bank of humanity.

BIBLIOGRAPHY

SURVEYS AND DESIGN IDEAS

Barnett, Arthur. *The Western Synagogue Through Two Centuries.* London: Valentine Mitchell Publishers, 1961.

Bates, Kenneth F. *Basic Design: Principles and Practice.* Cleveland: World Publications, 1960.

Child, Heather, and Colles, Dorothy. *Christian Symbols, Ancient and Modern.* London: G. Bell and Sons, 1972.

Dayan, Ruth. *Crafts of Israel.* New York: Macmillan Publishing Co. Inc., 1974.

Dean, Beryl. *Ecclesiastical Embroidery.* London: B.T. Batsford Ltd., 1958.

———. *Church Needlework.* London: B.T. Batsford Ltd., 1961.

———. *Ideas for Church Embroidery.* London: B.T. Batsford Ltd., 1968.

Freehof, Lillian, and King, Bucky. *Embroideries and Fabrics for the Synagogue and Home.* New York: Hearthside Press, 1967.

Hinz, Bill and Jim, and Meilach, Dona Z. *How to Create Your Own Designs.* New York: Doubleday Publishing Company, 1975.

Ireland, Marion. *Textile Art in the Church.* Nashville, Tennessee: Abingdon Press, 1966.

Kampf, Avram. *Contemporary Synagogue Art.* Philadelphia: Jewish Publication Society, 1966.

Langer, Suzanne K. *Problems of Art.* New York: Charles Scribner's Sons, 1957.

Malcolm, Dorothea. *Design Elements and Principles.* Worcester, Massachusetts: Davis Publications, 1972.

Papaneck, Victor. *Design for the Real World.* New York: Pantheon Books, Inc., 1971.

Strassfeld, Michael et al. *The Jewish Catalog: A Do-It-Yourself Kit.* Philadelphia: Jewish Publication Society, 1973.

FIBER

Aiken, Joyce, and Laury, Jean Ray. *Creating Body Coverings.* New York: Van Nostrand Reinhold Company, 1973.

Blumenau, Lili. *Creative Design in Wall Hangings.* New York: Crown Publishers, Inc., 1967.

Chamberlain, Marcia, and Crockett, Candace. *Beyond Weaving.* New York: Watson-Guptill Publications, 1974.

Conner, Margaret. *Introducing Fabric Collage.* London: B.T. Batsford, 1969.

Dendel, Esther. *Needleweaving—Easy As Embroidery.* New York: Doubleday and Co. Inc., 1971.

Harvey, Virginia. *Macrame: The Art of Creative Knotting.* New York: Van Nostrand Reinhold Company, 1967.

King, Bucky. *Creative Canvas Embroidery.* New York: Hearthside Press, 1963.

Kliot, Jules and Kaethe. *Bobbin Lace.* New York: Crown Publishers, Inc., 1973.

Laury, Jean Ray. *Applique Stitchery.* New York: Van Nostrand Reinhold Company, 1973.

Lillow, Ira. *Introducing Machine Embroidery.* New York: Watson-Guptill Publications, 1967.

McGrath, Lee P., and Scobey, Joan. *Do-It-All-Yourself Needlepoint.* New York: Simon and Schuster, Inc., 1971.

Plath, Iona. *Handweaving.* New York: Charles Scribner's Sons, 1964.

Rainey, Sarita. *Weaving Without a Loom.* Worcester, Massachusetts: Davis Publications, 1966.

Wilson, Jean. *Weaving is for Everyone.* New York: Van Nostrand Reinhold Company, 1967.

Zamierowski, Nell. *Step by Step Weaving.* Western Publishing Co., Inc., 1967.

BATIK, DYEING, TEXTILE PRINTING

Bystrom, Ellen. *Printing on Fabric.* New York: Van Nostrand Reinhold Company, 1972.

Kinsey, Anthony. *Introducing Screen Printing.* New York: Watson-Guptill Publications, 1972.

Krevitsky, Nik. *Batik Art and Craft.* Van Nostrand Reinhold Company, 1964.

Meilach, Dona Z. *Contemporary Batik and Tie-Dyeing.* New York: Crown Publishers, Inc., 1973.

Russ, Stephen. *Fabric Printing by Hands.* New York: Watson-Guptill Publications, 1964.

WOOD

Beecroft, Glynis. *Carving Techniques.* New York: Watson-Guptill Publications, 1977.

Dawson, Robert. *Practical Carving.* New York: Watson-Guptill Publications, 1977.

Gross, Chaim. *Wood Sculpture.* New York: Arco Publishing Company, Inc., 1965.

Meilach, Dona Z. *Contemporary Art with Wood: Creative Techniques and Appreciations.* New York: Crown Publishers, Inc., 1974.

Sack, Walter. *Woodcarving.* New York: Van Nostrand Reinhold Company, 1972.

Skinner, Freda. *Wood Carving.* New York: Bonanza Books. 1961.

Sommer, Elyse and Mike. *Creating with Driftwood.* New York: Crown Publishers, Inc., 1974.

Willcox, Donald J. *New Design in Wood.* New York: Van Nostrand Reinhold Company, 1970.

———. *Wood Design.* New York: Watson-Guptill Publications, 1977.

CERAMICS

Ball, F. Careton, and Lovoos, Janice S. *Making Pottery Without a Wheel.* New York: Van Nostrand Reinhold Company, 1965.

Chappell, James. *The Potter's Complete Book of Glazes.* New York: Watson-Guptill Publications, 1976.

Counts, Charles. *Pottery Workshop.* New York: Macmillan Publishing Co., Inc., 1973.

Fraser, Harry. *Glazes for the Craft Potter.* New York: Watson-Guptill Publications, 1973.

Hammer, Frank and Janet. *Clays.* New York: Watson-Guptill Publications, 1977.

Lucchest, Bruno, and Malmstrom, Margit. *Terracotta.* New York: Watson-Guptill Publications, 1968.

Reyntiens, Patrick. *The Technique of Stained Glass.* New York: Watson-Guptill Publications, 1977.

Rhodes, Daniel. *Clay and Glazes for the Potter.* Radnor, Pennsylvania: Chilton Book Company, 1957.

———. *Stoneware and Porcelain: The Art of High Fired Pottery.* Radnor, Pennsylvania: Chilton Book Company, 1959.

Rothenberg, Polly. *Complete Book of Ceramic Art.* New York: Crown Publishers Inc., 1972.

Schuler, Frederic. *Flameworking: Glassmaking for the Craftsman.* Radnor, Pennsylvania: Chilton Book Company, 1968.

Wood, Paul. *Stained Glass Crafting.* New York: Sterling Publishing Co., Inc., 1963.

MOSAICS

Berry, John. *Making Mosaics.* New York: Watson-Guptill Publications, 1966.

Lauppi, Walter. *Mosaics with Natural Stones.* New York: Sterling Publishing Co., Inc., 1974.

Lovoos, Janice, and Paramore, Felice. *Modern Mosaic Techniques.* New York: Watson-Guptill Publications, 1967.

Stribling, Mary-Lou. *Mosaic Techniques: New Aspects of Fragmented Design.* New York: Crown Publishers, Inc., 1966.

ENAMELS

Franklin, Geoffrey. *Simple Enamelling.* New York: Watson-Guptill Publications, 1977.

Harper, William. *Enamelling Step-by-Step.* Western Publishing Co., Inc., 1973.

Lammer, Jutta. *Make Your Own Enamels.* New York: Watson-Guptill Publications, 1968.

JEWELRY AND METALWORK

Baxter, William T. *Jewelry, Gem Cutting, and Metalcraft.* New York: McGraw-Hill Book Company, 1966.

Chamberlain, Marcia. *Metal Jewelry Techniques.* New York: Watson-Guptill Publications, 1977.

Morton, Philip. *Contemporary Jewelry.* New York: Holt, Rinehart and Winston, Inc., 1969.

Untrucht, Oppi. *Metal Techniques for Craftsmen.* New York: Doubleday and Co., 1968.

Von Newman, Robert. *The Design and Creation of Jewelry.* Radnor, Pennsylvania: Chilton Book Company, 1974.

PERIODICALS

Craft Horizons
Fiberarts
Shuttle, Spindle, and Dyepot
The Working Craftsman
Ceramics Monthly

DIRECTORY OF ARTISTS AND RELIGIOUS COMMUNITIES

The Reverend Kent E. Schneider, Director
Center for Contemporary Celebration
West Lafayette, Indiana

Religious Communities for the Arts
287 Park Ave. South
New York, N.Y. 10010

INDEX

Note: Page numbers in italics indicate illustrations.

alms bags, 44
alms basin, 27
alms boxes, 62
altar, 26
altar candlesticks, *35*
altar cloth, 44, *101*
altar cross, 30
altar frontals, *42-43, 86, 94, 96*
altar rail, 26
altar rugs and kneelers, *26-27*
ambry, 28
"Angel," *96*
angels, *14-15, 96, 116-17, 120*
animals, symbolic use of, 14, 18, *19, 23, 95, 105*
appliqué, *82, 93, 96, 101, 109-17*
ark, 28, *29*
ark curtains, 44
articles, traditional religious symbolic, 9-15

banners, *107-14*
baptismal font, 26, 62
"Betrayal, Supper, Death," *123*
Bible cover, *101*
book bindings, 42, 46
brazing, 80
bridal headdress, *102*
"Brotherhood," 58-59, *96*
"Brown Moon," *96*
burse and veil, 44, *45, 93*

calligraphy, *see* letters, symbolic use of
casting, 77
ceramics, 55-62, *96*
    the nonproduction potter, 62
    the production potter, 60

challah and matzoh covers, 46
champlevé, 74
chancel light, 35
Chanukah lights, 35, 62
chasuble, *38, 102-106*
Chi-Rho, 21, *22, 78*
"Chrismon," *83*
Christ, *33,* 126
    images of, as a symbol, 12, *34*
"Christ Glorified," *119*
Christmas candleholders, 62
chuppah, 30
church as a symbol, the, 15
clay for religious articles, 48
clergy and the craftsman:
    finding the craftsman, 49-51
    opportunities for the craftsman, 52-54
cloisonné, 74, *75-76*
cock, symbolic use of the, 18
color and symbolism, *83, 85*
    common associations, 8
    Hebrew liturgical, 6-7
    liturgical color chart, 7-8
Communion vessels, 36
"Continuation," *96*
contract between clergy and craftsman, 54
cope, *39*
corporal, 44
craftsmen:
    advertising flyers and, 50, 53
    as consultants, 53
    finding, for commissions, 49-51
    guidelines for submitting religious-oriented work, 53-54
cross, the, *9-11, 23, 33,* 62, *66, 71-73, 77, 96,* 118, *119.*
    121-22
crown as a symbol, the, 15, *41*
"Crown of Thorns," 56

dalmatic, *40, 105*
"Descent from the Cross, The," *66*
direct enamel, 74
disciples of Jesus, symbols for the, 16, *114*
"Dona Nobis Pacem," *65*
dossal, 34
dove, symbolic use of the, 18, *23*

eagle, symbolic use of the, 18
ecclesiastical appointments, 24–48
    chart of, by their use, 25
    furniture, 24, 25, *26–30*, 121
    general worship, articles for, 40–*45*, *69–71*, 76, *79*,
        84–86. 89–94. 96, 101
    individual worship, articles for, 45–*46*, *72-73*, *75-77*, 101
    lighting, 25, *35*, 60, 62, *65*
    materials used for, 47–48
    vessels, 25, 36, 62, *66*, 77, *80-81*, *96, 101*
    vesture, 25, 36–*40*, 45, *46*, *72*, *75*, *87-88*, *96, 102-106*
    wall decorations, *11, 23*, 25, *30-34*, *83-84*, *95*, 96, *102,*
        107-17, 119-24
embroidery, 82, *87-90*, *93*, *96, 101, 109-17*
enamel for religious articles, 47, 48, *62*, 64–80
    combined with metals, *63*, 65, *67*, 74–75, *96*
    techniques for enameling, 64–65
    terminology, 74
Eternal Light, 12, 35
Eucharist, *9*, 14, *67*
Eucharistic vessels, 36
Eucharistic vesture, 38–39
Evangelists, symbols for the, 17, *27*
"Everlasting Light," 56

fabricating, 80
"Family," 61
"Festival of Holidays," *124-25*
festivals, colors symbolic of religious, 7–8
fiber for religious articles, 47–48, 82–*115*
fish, symbolic use of the, *14*, 18, *19, 23*, 95, *105*
"Fishers of Men," *114*
"Fishes and Loaves," *14, 26*
flyers, advertising, 50, 53
forging, 77, *79-80*
"Fourteen Stations of the Cross," 34
funeral pall, 44
furniture as religious art objects, 24, 25, *26-30*, *78*, 121

general worship, religious art objects used for, 25, 40–*45*,
    69-71, 76, *79*, *84-86*, *89-94*, *96, 101*
Gill, Dr. Theodore, 126
glass for religious articles, 48

"Hanging Menorah II," *84*
hart, symbolic use of the, 18
Holy Ark as a symbol, 12
Holy Spirit as a symbol, 12
"Honor of our Fathers, In," 69

Indiana, Robert, 20
individual worship, religious art objects used for, 25, 45–*46*,
    72-73, 75-77, 101
"Interplay," 102
interview of craftsman by clergy, 53
"Iron Cross," *71*

"Jesus is Lain in the Tomb," *112*
jewelry:
    used in private worship, 45, *46, 72, 75, 76, 77, 96*
    worn by clergy, 40
John, symbol for, 17, *27*

lamb, symbolic use of the, 18
lavabo, 62
leather religious articles, 48, *114*
Le Corbusier, 149
lecturn, 28
lecturn hangings, *9*, 42
"Le Pere," *66*
letters, symbolic use of, 20-21, *22, 30, 41, 76, 78, 79, 81,*
    87, 96, 112, 113
lighting as religious art objects, 25, 35, 60, 62, *65*
lion, symbolic use of the, 18
"Lord Delights in You, The," *111*
"Lot's Wife," *108*
Luke, *20*
    symbol for, 17, *27*

macramé, 82, *94, 104, 117*
"Madonna and Child," *31*
Mark, symbol for, 17, *27*
"Martyrs and Fighters," *63*
Matisse, Henri, 49
Matthew, symbol for, 17, *27*
"Meditation I," *122*
menorah, 12, *13*, 30, 56, 60, 62, *69-70*, *84*, 96
metal for religious articles, 47, 64–84, *96, 101*
    combined with enameling techniques, *63*, 65, *67*,
    74-75, 96
    terminology, 77
"Metamorphosis," *117*
mezuzah, *46, 75, 76*
Michelangelo, 49
miter, *39*

mixed media, 122–*23*
"Multitude, The," *95*

"Nativity," *123*
Nativity, 12, *32*, 62, *113*, *123*

pall, 45
"Parable of the Sower," *107*
peacock, symbolic use of the, 18
pelican, symbolic use of the, 18
"Perchance to Dream," *116–17*
phylacteries, 38
piscina, 62
plants, symbolic use of, 18–19, *85*, *87*
plastic religious articles, 48
plique-à-jour, 74, *96*
portfolio, craftsman's, 53
printing, wood block, *123*
pulpit, 28
pulpit falls, 42, *84–85*, *91–92*
purificator, 45
pyx, 62

ram, symbolic use of the, 18
Raphael, 49
"Reliquary," *75*
rugs and kneelers, *26–27*

"St. Andrew," *120*
"St. Francis of Assisi," *59*
"St. John and Angel," *120*
"St. Matthew," *121*
St. Paul, symbol for, 16
St. Peter's, Rome, Italy, 64
sculpture, *116–17*, 122
seating, 28
Seder vessels, 36, 62
Shahn, Ben, 20
ship as a symbol, the, 15
soldering, 80
Solomon, King, 126
star, six-pointed, as a symbol, 15, *88*
stations of the cross, 34
stone for religious articles, 47
submission sheets, 54
surplice, 36
Sutherland, Graham, 49
symbolism in religious art, 6–*22*
    animals and plants, 18–*19*, *85*, *87*, *95*, *105*
    color, 6–8, *83*, *85*
    letters, 20–*22*, *30*, *41*, *87*, *112*, *113*

prophets, patriarchs, and gospels, 16–17, *27*, *114*
traditional religious articles, 9–15, *23*

tallis, *37*, *87*
tallis bag, *88*
tapestry weaving, 82, *83*
"Te Deum," *62*
tefillin bag, 38
Ten Commandments as a symbol, 15
Tetragrammaton, 20
Torah binder, 42, *70*, *90*
Torah mantel, 40, *41*, *89*
Torah pointer, 42, *76*, *79*
Torah shield or breastplate, *69*, *79*
towels, 44
Tree of Life as a symbol, 9, *29*, *42*, *79*, *96*, 118
tribes of Israel, symbols for the twelve, 17, *79*
Trinity, 12, *13*, *66*, *83*, *101*

Urban VIII, Pope, 49

vases, flower, 36, 60
veil and burse, 44, *45*, *93*
"Veronica Wipes the Face of Jesus," *112*
vessels as religious art objects, 25, 36, 62, *66*, *77*, *80–81*,
    96, *101*
vesture as religious art objects, 25, 36–*40*, *87*, *102–106*
"Virgin and Child," *59*
Virgin Mary as a symbol, 12

"Waiting for Elijah," *77*
wall decorations as religious art objects, *11*, *23*, 25, *30–34*,
    83–84, *95*, *96*, *102*, *107–17*, *119–24*
water as a symbol, 12
Westminster Abbey, England, 64
"What We Preach," *115*
windows, 28, *29*
"Woman Clothed With Sun," *115*
wood, religious articles made from, 47, *61*, 118–24
    nonproduction woodworkers, 122–24
    production woodworkers, 121
    types of, 118

"You Can't Beat God for Imagination," *110*